Longman School
Shakespeare

Othello

Editor: John O'Connor
Textual Consultant: Dr Stewart Eames

Volume Editor: John O'Connor

GCSE Assessment Practice:
Chris Sutcliffe (AQA)
Pam Taylor (Edexcel)
Margaret Graham (WJEC)

Integrated Learning Resources Centre
Greenwich Community College
95 Plumstead Road
London SE18 7DQ

Longman is an imprint of Pearson Education Limited, a company incorporated in England and Wales, having its registered office at Edinburgh Gate, Harlow, Essex, CM20 2JE. Registered company number: 872828

www.pearsonschoolsandfecolleges.co.uk

Longman is a registered trademark of Pearson Education Limited

The rights of Dr Stewart Eames, John O'Connor, Chris Sutcliffe, Pam Taylor and Margaret Graham to be identified as the authors of this work have been asserted by them in accordance with the Copyright, Designs and Patent Act 1988.

First published 2005
This new edition published 2010

15
10 9 8 7 6

British Library Cataloguing in Publication Data
A catalogue record for this book is available from the British Library

ISBN 978 1 4082 3688 8

Typeset by Juice Creative Ltd, Hertfordshire
Cover photo © Photostage Ltd
Printed and bound in Malaysia (CTP-VVP)

We are grateful to the following for permission to reproduce copyright material:

Photographs
Alamy: *page 253*, Adrian Chinery ; Getty Images: *page 251* Andrea Pistolesi/ The Image Bank

Every effort has been made to contact copyright holders of material reproduced in this book. Any omissions will be rectified in subsequent printings if notice is given to the publishers.

CONTENTS

ACT 1: SCENE BY SCENE

1 Roderigo is angry that Iago did not tell him that Desdemona and Othello have married in secret. Iago says that he knew nothing about it and that he hates Othello for promoting Cassio to be his new lieutenant. Iago and Roderigo wake Desdemona's father, Brabantio, and tell him what his daughter has done. Brabantio is furious and sends out search parties to look for her.

2 Pretending to be concerned, Iago warns Othello that Brabantio is furious about his marriage to Desdemona. Cassio enters and tells Othello that the Duke wants to see him on urgent state business. Othello sets off to see the Duke but is met by Brabantio who tries to have him arrested for stealing his daughter.

3 When Othello and Brabantio arrive to see the Duke, he and his council are discussing reports that a Turkish fleet has set sail for Cyprus. Brabantio accuses Othello of stealing Desdemona, but she confirms Othello's account of their love. The Duke gives Othello command of Cyprus and orders him to leave that night. Iago convinces Roderigo that Desdemona will soon get tired of Othello and persuades him to follow the couple to Cyprus. Alone, Iago plots to destroy their happiness.

ACT 2: SCENE BY SCENE

1 A storm has destroyed the invading Turkish fleet, but the ships from Venice arrive safely in Cyprus. Iago tells Roderigo that Desdemona is having an affair with Cassio. He persuades Roderigo to help him make Cassio lose his job.

2 Festivities are announced to celebrate the defeat of the Turks.

3 Iago gets Cassio drunk and, with Roderigo's help, involves him in a fight. Cassio wounds Montano and Othello sacks him. Iago persuades Cassio to ask Desdemona to help him get his job back. He hopes that this will help make Othello believe that Desdemona is having an affair with Cassio.

ACT 3: SCENE BY SCENE

1 Emilia promises to arrange a meeting with Desdemona for Cassio so that he can ask for her help in getting his job back.

2 Othello begins an inspection of the fortress's defences.

3 When Othello and Iago see Cassio talking with Desdemona, Iago tries to make it look suspicious. However, Desdemona openly tells Othello about her talk with Cassio and begs Othello to take him back as lieutenant. Iago tries again to make Othello suspicious of Cassio. Othello begins to doubt Desdemona's love for him. Thinking that Othello is unwell, Desdemona tries to bind his head with a precious handkerchief that Othello gave her, but he rejects her and she drops the handkerchief. Emilia picks it up and gives it to Iago. Othello is suspicious, but does not want to believe that Desdemona has been unfaithful. Angrily, he turns on Iago and demands proof. Iago lies, saying that Cassio talked in his sleep about Desdemona and claims that he has seen Cassio with her handkerchief. Othello is convinced by Iago's story and both men take a vow: Othello to take revenge on Desdemona and Iago to kill Cassio.

4 When Othello demands to see her handkerchief, Desdemona has to make excuses as she has lost it. She turns the subject to Cassio, and Othello reacts angrily. Emilia suspects that he is jealous. Cassio asks his girlfriend, Bianca, to copy the embroidery in the handkerchief that he has found in his room, not realising that it belongs to Desdemona.

ACT 4: SCENE BY SCENE

1 Provoked by Iago's descriptions of Desdemona's infidelity, Othello has a seizure. When he comes round, Iago persuades Othello to hide and watch his conversation with Cassio. Iago jokes with Cassio about Bianca, knowing that Othello will think they are talking about Desdemona. Bianca arrives and accuses Cassio of accepting the handkerchief from another woman, which seems to Othello like final proof of Desdemona's guilt. He is so enraged that he strikes Desdemona when she arrives with Lodovico. Iago tells Lodovico that this is typical of Othello's behaviour.

2 Othello questions Emilia about Desdemona's friendship with Cassio, but is so convinced of her guilt he dismisses Emilia's answers. When Othello calls Desdemona a whore, Emilia tries to comfort her, realising that someone must have poisoned Othello's mind against her. Roderigo is angry that he has not yet won Desdemona, as Iago promised. Iago tells Roderigo that Othello will shortly leave Cyprus with Desdemona, leaving Cassio in charge. Iago persuades Roderigo that if he kills Cassio, he will prevent Othello and Desdemona from leaving Cyprus.

3 As Desdemona prepares for bed, she sings a mournful song. She and Emilia talk about men and women.

ACT 5: SCENE BY SCENE

1 In a late-night attack, Roderigo wounds Cassio, but is himself stabbed by Iago, and later dies. When Lodovico and Gratiano arrive, Iago accuses Bianca of being involved in the attack on Cassio.

2 Othello enters Desdemona's bedroom, preparing to kill her. When she wakes, he accuses her of having an affair with Cassio. Though Desdemona protests her innocence and begs for her life, Othello smothers her. Emilia arrives to report the attack on Cassio and sees Desdemona die. Othello admits that he killed her. Emilia's cries bring Montano, Gratiano and Iago to the bedroom. Othello tries to explain his actions but when Emilia reveals that she gave the handkerchief to Iago, Othello realises that Desdemona was an innocent victim of Iago's plot. Iago kills Emilia and tries to escape, but is caught. Lodovico and Cassio arrive and the full extent of Iago's plot becomes clear. Othello kills himself and Lodovico gives orders for Iago to be tortured.

VISITORS TO CYPRUS

OTHELLO
An African-born general in the army of Venice
He is sent to take command of Cyprus which is under threat from the Turks. Iago tricks him into believing that Desdemona is having an affair with Cassio.

DESDEMONA
Othello's wife
She marries Othello in secret. She later begs Othello to give Cassio back his position as lieutenant.

CASSIO
Othello's new lieutenant
Iago gets him drunk so that he loses his position as lieutenant. Iago later plants Desdemona's handkerchief in his room.

IAGO
Othello's standard-bearer (lower in rank than lieutenant)
He is angry that Othello has made Cassio lieutenant instead of him and vows revenge on both men.

EMILIA
Iago's wife and Desdemona's companion
She gives Desdemona's handkerchief to Iago.

LODOVICO
An important Venetian nobleman and a relative of Brabantio
He sees Othello strike Desdemoana and finds letters in Roderigo's pockets that reveal Iago's plots.

GRATIANO
Brabantio's brother
He and Lodovico assist Cassio after Roderigo has attacked him.

RODERIGO
A rich young Venetian in love with Desdemona
He follows Othello and Desdemona to Cyprus. Iago pretends to be helping him win Desdemona's love, but is really using him in his plot.

CLOWN
Othello's servant

THE DUKE OF VENICE AND HIS COUNCIL

THE DUKE
The person of highest rank in Venice
He tries to calm Brabantio when
he complains about Desdemona's
marriage to Othello. He sends
Othello to take command of the
defence of Cyprus.

BRABANTIO
Desdemona's father and a Senator.
He is angry and bitter that his
daughter has deceived him by
secretly marrying Othello.

SENATORS
Members of the Duke's council
They discuss the reports concerning
the Turkish invasion fleet and listen
to Othello and Desdemona tell the
Duke how they fell in love.

OFFICER
An official in the council chamber

SAILOR AND MESSENGER
They bring conflicting reports about
the Turkish fleet.

RESIDENTS OF CYPRUS

MONTANO
*Governor of Cyprus before
Othello arrives*
He is wounded by the drunken
Cassio.

BIANCA
Cassio's girlfriend on Cyprus
Cassio asks her to copy the
embroidery on the handkerchief
that Iago has dropped in his room.
Iago accuses her of being involved
in the attack on Cassio.

GENTLEMEN
They anxiously await the safe arrival
of Othello on Cyprus in the storm
that has destroyed the Turkish fleet.

HERALD

MUSICIANS

VISITORS TO CYPRUS

OTHELLO *the 'Moor', a general in the army of Venice*

DESDEMONA *Othello's wife and Brabantio's daughter*

IAGO *Othello's standard-bearer*

EMILIA *Iago's wife*

CASSIO *Othello's lieutenant*

RODERIGO *a Venetian gentleman*

LODOVICO *a high-ranking Venetian nobleman, related to Brabantio*

GRATIANO *Brabantio's brother*

a **CLOWN** *Othello's servant*

THE DUKE OF VENICE AND HIS COUNCIL

DUKE OF VENICE

BRABANTIO *a Venetian senator, Desdemona's father*

SENATORS, OFFICERS, SERVANTS *to Brabantio and* **ATTENDANTS**

SAILOR

MESSENGER

RESIDENTS OF CYPRUS

MONTANO *Governor of Cyprus*

BIANCA *Cassio's girlfriend*

HERALD

GENTLEMEN, MUSICIANS, ATTENDANTS *and* **OFFICERS**

Act 1 takes place in Venice. The rest of the play takes place on the island of Cyprus.

In this scene ...

- Iago tells Roderigo that he hates Othello and is angry that he has not been made Othello's lieutenant.
- Iago and Roderigo inform Brabantio that his daughter, Desdemona, has run off with Othello.
- Brabantio is furious and orders his servants to search for Desdemona.

Roderigo complains to Iago that he did not tell him about Desdemona's relationship with Othello. Iago says that he hates the Moor and is angry that Othello has made Cassio lieutenant instead of him.

THINK ABOUT for GCSE

Structure and form
- The play opens in the middle of a conversation. What are they talking about? What is Roderigo angry about? Who, according to Roderigo, does Iago hate and why might he hate him?

Characterisation
- Iago mentions a man called Cassio. What does he say about him in lines 17 to 25?

Context
- In the time when *Othello* is set, there was a great rivalry between different states in the region that is now modern Italy. In what tone might Iago say line 18?

1 **Tush ... me**: Rubbish! Don't give me that!
3 **the strings ... thine**: you had control of it
4 **'Sblood**: God's blood (an oath)
5 **abhor**: hate
7 **great ones**: important people
8 **suit**: request
9 **Off-capped**: removed their hats in respect
12 **Evades**: avoids answering directly
    bombast circumstance: long-winded excuse
13 **epithets of war**: military language
15 **Non-suits my mediators**: turns down the people pleading on my behalf
    Certes: Certainly
17 **Forsooth**: Truly
    arithmetician: theorist
21 **division**: planning / strategy
22 **bookish theoric**: theory from books
23 **togèd consuls**: senators in their peace-time robes
24 **Mere ... practice**: i.e. He's all talk
25 **had th' election**: was chosen
27 **grounds**: battlefields
28 **belee'd and calmed**: prevented from getting on
29 **debitor ... counter-caster**: i.e. office-worker (further slurs at Cassio's lack of experience as a soldier)
31 **bless ... mark**: help us
    his Moorship: 'his worship the Moor' (i.e. Othello)
    ancient: standard-bearer (lower in rank than lieutenant)

Venice: a street (near Brabantio's house) at night.

Enter RODERIGO *and* IAGO.

RODERIGO   Tush – never tell me! I take it much unkindly
That thou, Iago, who hast had my purse
As if the strings were thine, shouldst know of this.

IAGO   'Sblood, but you'll not hear me! If ever I did dream
Of such a matter, abhor me.

RODERIGO   Thou told'st me   5
Thou didst hold him in thy hate.

IAGO   Despise me
If I do not! Three great ones of the city,
In personal suit to make me his lieutenant,
Off-capped to him. And by the faith of man,
I know my price: I am worth no worse a place.   10
But he, as loving his own pride and purposes,
Evades them with a bombast circumstance,
Horribly stuffed with epithets of war –
And, in conclusion,
Non-suits my mediators. For, 'Certes,' says he,   15
'I have already chose my officer.' And what was he?
Forsooth, a great arithmetician,
One Michael Cassio, a Florentine,
(A fellow almost damned in a fair wife)
That never set a squadron in the field,   20
Nor the division of a battle knows
More than a spinster – unless the bookish theoric,
Wherein the togèd consuls can propose
As masterly as he. Mere prattle without practice
Is all his soldiership. But he, sir, had th' election!   25
And I, of whom his eyes had seen the proof
At Rhodes, at Cyprus, and on other grounds
Christian and heathen, must be belee'd and calmed
By debitor and creditor. This counter-caster,
He, in good time, must his lieutenant be,   30
And I – God bless the mark! – his Moorship's ancient.

Iago tells Roderigo that he will only stay in Othello's service to get what he wants out of him.

33 **service**: life as a soldier
34 **Preferment**: promotion
    letter and affection: who you know and favouritism
35 **old gradation**: traditional step-by-step promotion
37 **affined**: duty-bound

39 **content you**: don't worry
40 **serve my turn upon**: get what I want out of

43 **knee-crooking knave**: humbly bowing servant
44 **doting … bondage**: loving his position as an obedient servant
46 **provender**: animal feed
    cashiered: he is sacked
48 **trimmed … duty**: dressed up to look dutiful
49 **attending on**: looking after
51 **thrive**: succeed
    lined their coats: got what they can
52 **Do *themselves* homage**: look after themselves

THINK ABOUT *for* GCSE

Language
• Iago's language is often confusing. What do you think he means by 'Were I the Moor, I would not be Iago' (line 56) and 'I am not what I am' (line 64)?

Characterisation
• What do we learn about Iago's feelings and intentions from what he says to Roderigo in lines 39 to 64?

---

58 **not I for**: I don't do it for
59 **peculiar end**: private purposes

61 **native … heart**: true actions and intention
62 **complement extern**: outward show
63 **wear … sleeve**: show my feelings openly
64 **daws**: jackdaws
65 **full … owe**: lucky man Othello will be
66 **carry it thus**: get away with it

Roderigo	By heaven, I rather would have been his hangman!
Iago	Why, there's no remedy. 'Tis the curse of service:
	Preferment goes by letter and affection,
	And not by old gradation, where each second 35
	Stood heir to the first. Now, sir, be judge yourself,
	Whether I in any just term am affined
	To love the Moor.
Roderigo	I would not follow him then.
Iago	O, sir, content you.
	I follow him to serve my turn upon him. 40
	We cannot all be masters, nor all masters
	Cannot be truly followed. You shall mark
	Many a duteous and knee-crooking knave
	That, doting on his own obsequious bondage,
	Wears out his time, much like his master's ass, 45
	For naught but provender – and when he's old, cashiered.
	Whip me such honest knaves! Others there are
	Who, trimmed in forms and visages of duty,
	Keep yet their hearts attending on themselves,
	And, throwing but shows of service on their lords, 50
	Do well thrive by them – and when they have lined
	their coats
	Do *themselves* homage. These fellows have some soul –
	And such a one do I profess myself.
	For, sir,
	It is as sure as you are Roderigo, 55
	Were I the Moor, I would not be Iago.
	In following him, I follow but myself.
	Heaven is my judge, not I for love and duty,
	But seeming so, for my peculiar end.
	For when my outward action doth demonstrate 60
	The native act and figure of my heart
	In complement extern, 'tis not long after
	But I will wear my heart upon my sleeve
	For daws to peck at. I am not what I am.
Roderigo	What a full fortune does the thick-lips owe 65
	If he can carry it thus!

Iago persuades Roderigo to
wake Desdemona's father,
Brabantio, and tell him that she
has run away with Othello.

68 **Proclaim**: shout Brabantio's name
incense: infuriate
69 **though ... dwell**: i.e. he might be
having a good time now
70 **Plague ... flies**: i.e. ruin things for him
71 **throw ... vexation**: i.e. find
opportunities to harm him
72 **lose some colour**: be spoilt
74–6 **with ... spied**: like people shouting out
when they spot a house on fire in the
night

THINK ABOUT for GCSE

Structure and form
• How does the structure
of the verse in lines 66 to
72 help to add a sense of
urgency at this point?

Performance and staging
• Look at the stage direction
at line 80. How might this
part of the scene have been
performed on the stage of
Shakespeare's Globe? How
does the dialogue help the
audience to understand that
it is night and that Brabantio
cannot see who is calling to
him?

85 **Zounds**: By God's wounds (a powerful
oath)

88 **tupping**: having sex with
89 **snorting**: snoring
90 **grandsire**: grandfather

IAGO	Call up her father!
	Rouse him, make after him, poison his delight,
	Proclaim him in the streets, incense her kinsmen –
	And though he in a fertile climate dwell,
	Plague him with flies. Though that his joy be joy, **70**
	Yet throw such chances of vexation on't
	As it may lose some colour.
RODERIGO	Here is her father's house. I'll call aloud.
IAGO	Do – with like timorous accent and dire yell
	As when, by night and negligence, the fire **75**
	Is spied in populous cities.
RODERIGO	What, ho, Brabantio! Signior Brabantio, ho!
IAGO	Awake! What ho, Brabantio! Thieves, thieves!
	Look to your house, your daughter, and your bags!
	Thieves, thieves! **80**

BRABANTIO *appears above, at a window.*

BRABANTIO	What is the reason of this terrible summons?
	What is the matter there?
RODERIGO	Signior, is all your family within?
IAGO	Are your doors locked?
BRABANTIO	Why, wherefore ask you this?
IAGO	Zounds, sir, y'are robbed! For shame, put on your gown! **85**
	Your heart is burst, you have lost half your soul.
	Even now, now, very now, an old black ram
	Is tupping your white ewe. Arise, arise!
	Awake the snorting citizens with the bell,
	Or else the devil will make a grandsire of you. **90**
	Arise I say!
BRABANTIO	What, have you lost your wits?
RODERIGO	Most reverend signior, do you know my voice?
BRABANTIO	Not I – what are you?
RODERIGO	My name is Roderigo.

Iago and Roderigo inform Brabantio that his daughter has run off with Othello. Iago takes care to keep himself hidden from Brabantio.

95   **charged**: ordered

97   **for thee**: going to marry you
98   **distemp'ring draughts**: i.e. alcohol
99   **Upon malicious knavery**: aiming to cause trouble
100 **start my quiet**: disturb my rest

102 **spirits**: character
     place: position as senator
103 **make … thee**: cause you a lot of trouble

105 **grange**: isolated farmhouse

108 **service**: a good turn

110 **covered with**: have sex with
     Barbary: from north Africa
     nephews: descendants
111 **coursers**: fast horses
112 **jennets for germans**: horses as relatives
113 **profane**: foul-mouthed
115 **making … backs**: i.e. having sex

118 **beseech**: beg

121 **At … night**: i.e. just after midnight
123 **knave … hire**: servant who could be hired by anybody
     gondolier: canal boatman

THINK ABOUT for GCSE

Themes and issues

- **Race**: Roderigo earlier called Othello 'the thick-lips' (line 65). What other examples of racist language have Roderigo and Iago used when referring to Othello? Look at lines 85 to 91 and 107 to 112.

Language

- How does Iago choose his words in order to make Brabantio angry? Look at the alliteration in lines 110 to 112 and Brabantio's reply in line 116, for example.

- What does Iago's imagery tell us about his attitude towards sex? Look at lines 87 to 88, 109 to 110 and 114 to 115, for example.

BRABANTIO	The worser welcome!
	I have charged thee not to haunt about my doors. 95
	In honest plainness thou hast heard me say
	My daughter is not for thee. And now, in madness,
	Being full of supper and distemp'ring draughts,
	Upon malicious knavery dost thou come
	To start my quiet. 100
RODERIGO	Sir, sir, sir –
BRABANTIO	But thou must needs be sure
	My spirits and my place have in them power
	To make this bitter to thee.
RODERIGO	Patience, good sir.
BRABANTIO	What tell'st thou me of robbing? This is Venice;
	My house is not a grange.
RODERIGO	Most grave Brabantio, 105
	In simple and pure soul I come to you.
IAGO	Zounds, sir, you are one of those that will not serve God
	if the devil bid you! Because we come to do you service
	and you think we are ruffians, you'll have your daughter
	covered with a Barbary horse. You'll have your nephews 110
	neigh to you – you'll have coursers for cousins, and
	jennets for germans.
BRABANTIO	What profane wretch art thou?
IAGO	I am one, sir, that comes to tell you your daughter and
	the Moor are making the beast with two backs. 115
BRABANTIO	Thou art a villain!
IAGO	You are – a senator.
BRABANTIO	This thou shalt answer! I know thee, Roderigo.
RODERIGO	Sir, I will answer anything. But I beseech you,
	If't be your pleasure and most wise consent,
	(As partly I find it is) that your fair daughter, 120
	At this odd-even and dull watch o' the night,
	Transported with no worse nor better guard
	But with a knave of common hire, a gondolier,

While Brabantio goes to confirm that Desdemona is not in the house, Iago gives Roderigo further instructions and departs.

THINK ABOUT for GCSE

Language

• Look at Roderigo's language in his speech to Brabantio (lines 118 to 138). How does he try to build up Brabantio's fears about the man Desdemona has run away with? For example, compare his use of alliteration and adjectives as he describes Othello with the nouns he uses when talking about Desdemona.

Characterisation

• Why do you think Iago has gone to the trouble of informing Brabantio of his daughter's secret marriage, when he knows that it cannot do Othello any long-term harm (lines 145 to 151)?

124 **gross clasps**: disgusting embraces
     lascivious: lustful
125 **your allowance**: done with your permission
126 **saucy**: very rude
128 **We ... rebuke**: you have told us off unfairly
129 **from ... civility**: not knowing how to behave properly
130 **trifle ... reverence**: i.e. waste your time, sir
132 **revolt**: rebellion
134 **extravagant ... stranger**: i.e. foreigner with no fixed home
135 **Straight ... yourself**: Confirm it straight away
138 **Strike ... tinder**: i.e. Light the torches
139 **taper**: candle
140 **accident**: event

143 **meet**: fitting
     wholesome ... place: good for my position
144 **produced**: called as a witness
146 **gall**: annoy
     check: reprimand
147 **cast**: dismiss
148 **loud reason**: public support
149 **stands in act**: have begun
150 **fathom**: abilities

154 **sign**: appearance

156 **the Sagittary**: an inn (named after an archer in Greek mythology)

To the gross clasps of a lascivious Moor –
If this be known to you, and your allowance, **125**
We then have done you bold and saucy wrongs.
But if you know not this, my manners tell me
We have your wrong rebuke. Do not believe
That from the sense of all civility
I thus would play and trifle with your reverence. **130**
Your daughter, if you have not given her leave,
I say again, hath made a gross revolt –
Tying her duty, beauty, wit, and fortunes
In an extravagant and wheeling stranger
Of here and everywhere. Straight satisfy yourself. **135**
If she be in her chamber, or your house,
Let loose on me the justice of the state
For thus deluding you.

BRABANTIO   Strike on the tinder, ho!
Give me a taper! Call up all my people!
This accident is not unlike my dream. **140**
Belief of it oppresses me already.
Light, I say! Light!

Exit above.

IAGO   Farewell, for I must leave you.
It seems not meet, nor wholesome to my place,
To be produced – as, if I stay, I shall –
Against the Moor. For I do know the state, **145**
However this may gall him with some check,
Cannot with safety cast him – for he's embarked
With such loud reason to the Cyprus wars,
Which even now stands in act, that for their souls
Another of his fathom they have none **150**
To lead their business. In which regard,
Though I do hate him as I do hell-pains,
Yet, for necessity of present life,
I must show out a flag and sign of love,
Which is indeed but sign. That you shall surely find him, **155**
Lead to the Sagittary the raisèd search,
And there will I be with him. So farewell.

Exit.

Brabantio finds that Desdemona is gone and orders his servants to search for her. Roderigo says he knows where she and Othello are.

159   despisèd time: hateful old age

THINK ABOUT for GCSE

Characterisation

- What do we learn about Brabantio here? Think about what he says about his dreams, his daughter, love-potions or spells and Roderigo.

- What have we learned so far which shows Roderigo to be a classic 'gull' (a rich fool who is easily tricked by a clever schemer)? Look at lines 1 to 3, for example, and Iago's use of Roderigo in this scene.

Themes and issues

- In what ways does this opening scene introduce the theme of **truth and deception**? For example, as far as you can tell, which of Iago's statements have been truths and which lies? What has he said that might well have confused the slow-witted Roderigo?

167   treason ... blood: rebellion against her family
169   charms: love potions or spells
170   property: true nature
       maidhood: girlhood

173   would ... her: I wish you had married her
174   Some ... another: i.e. Send search-parties out in different directions
175   apprehend: arrest

179   command: call upon help

181   deserve your pains: reward you for your trouble

Re-enter BRABANTIO *below, in his nightgown. Servants with him carry burning torches.*

BRABANTIO	It is too true an evil. Gone she is –
	And what's to come of my despisèd time
	Is naught but bitterness. Now Roderigo, 160
	Where didst thou see her? – O unhappy girl! –
	With the Moor, say'st thou? – Who would be a father? –
	How didst thou know 'twas she? – O, she deceives me
	Past thought! – What said she to you? – Get more
	tapers!
	Raise all my kindred! – Are they married, think you? 165
RODERIGO	Truly I think they are.
BRABANTIO	O heaven! How got she out? O treason of the blood!
	Fathers, from hence trust not your daughters' minds
	By what you see them act. Is there not charms
	By which the property of youth and maidhood 170
	May be abused? Have you not read, Roderigo,
	Of some such thing?
RODERIGO	Yes, sir, I have indeed.
BRABANTIO	Call up my brother. – O, would you had had her! –
	Some one way, some another. – Do you know
	Where we may apprehend her and the Moor? 175
RODERIGO	I think I can discover him, if you please
	To get good guard and go along with me.
BRABANTIO	Pray you lead on. At every house I'll call;
	I may command at most. – Get weapons, ho!
	And raise some special officers of night. – 180
	On, good Roderigo – I'll deserve your pains.

Exeunt.

In this scene ...

- As Othello discusses his marriage with Iago they are met by Cassio. He informs them that the Duke has sent urgently for Othello.
- Brabantio arrives and angrily accuses Othello of using magic to make Desdemona love him.

Iago pretends to be worried that Othello might be punished for marrying Desdemona. Othello is confident that his position and record of service as a general will protect him.

2 **very stuff**: essence
3 **contrived**: pre-planned / cold-blooded
3–4 **I lack ... service**: I'm sometimes too soft-hearted for my own good
5 **yerked**: stabbed

6 **prated**: said stupid things
7 **scurvy**: insulting

10 **did ... him**: had difficulty putting up with what he said
11 **fast**: i.e. properly
12 **magnifico**: chief nobleman (i.e. Brabantio)
13 **hath in ... potential**: could bring to bear a powerful influence
15 **grievance**: punishment
17 **give him cable**: allow him to do
18 **Signiory**: Venetian parliament
19 **out-tongue**: put up stronger arguments than
21 **promulgate**: announce
fetch ... being: am descended
22 **siege**: rank
demerits: merits / good qualities
23 **speak unbonneted**: be considered equal
25 **But that I**: if I did not
26 **unhousèd free condition**: unrestrained freedom
27 **Put into circumscription**: restrict
28 **yond**: over there

THINK ABOUT *for* **GCSE**

Performance and staging
- If you were the director, what first impression would you want the audience to have of Othello from his opening speeches?

Characterisation
- What information does Othello give in lines 17 to 28 about his reputation in Venice, his family background and the strength of his love for Desdemona?

Venice: another street.

Enter OTHELLO, IAGO, *and attendants with torches burning.*

IAGO	Though in the trade of war I have slain men,
	Yet do I hold it very stuff o' the conscience
	To do no contrived murder. I lack iniquity
	Sometimes to do me service. Nine or ten times
	I had thought t' have yerked him – here under the ribs. 5
OTHELLO	'Tis better as it is.
IAGO	Nay, but he prated –
	And spoke such scurvy and provoking terms
	Against your honour
	That, with the little godliness I have,
	I did full hard forbear him. But I pray you sir, 10
	Are you fast married? For be sure of this –
	That the magnifico is much beloved,
	And hath in his effect a voice potential
	As double as the Duke's. He will divorce you –
	Or put upon you what restraint or grievance 15
	The law, with all his might to enforce it on,
	Will give him cable.
OTHELLO	Let him do his spite.
	My services which I have done the Signiory
	Shall out-tongue his complaints. 'Tis yet to know –
	Which when I know that boasting is an honour 20
	I shall promulgate – I fetch my life and being
	From men of royal siege: and my demerits
	May speak unbonneted to as proud a fortune
	As this that I have reached. For know, Iago –
	But that I love the gentle Desdemona, 25
	I would not my unhousèd free condition
	Put into circumscription and confine
	For the seas' worth. But look – what lights come yond?
IAGO	These are the raisèd father and his friends.
	You were best go in.

Cassio brings news that the Duke wants to see Othello urgently on state business. Iago tells Cassio that Othello has got married.

31 **parts**: character / talents
title: legal right
perfect soul: clear conscience
32 **manifest me rightly**: show what I am
33 **Janus**: the two-faced Roman god

37 **haste-posthaste**: i.e. immediate

39 **divine**: guess
40 **heat**: urgency
41 **sequent**: following one after the other

43 **consuls**: senators
44 **hotly**: urgently

46 **several quests**: separate search parties

49 **Ancient**: Standard-bearer

50 **boarded**: 1 captured; 2 taken sexually
carrack: treasure ship

53 **Marry**: 1 by the Virgin Mary; 2 a play on 'marry'

THINK ABOUT for GCSE

Language
- What does Iago's reply to Cassio in lines 50 to 51 mean? What does the image suggest about Iago's attitude to Othello's marriage?

Performance and staging
- If you were the director at Shakespeare's Globe, how would you position the actors on the stage after Othello's exit? What would you take into account when placing (a) Iago and Cassio; and (b) the torch-carrying officers?
- Line 52 is split into three parts. How might the actors deliver it?

OTHELLO	Not I. I must be found.	30
	My parts, my title, and my perfect soul	
	Shall manifest me rightly. Is it they?	

Enter Cassio, *and Officers with more torches.*

| IAGO | By Janus, I think no! | |

OTHELLO	The servants of the Duke? And my lieutenant?	
	The goodness of the night upon you, friends!	35
	What is the news?	

CASSIO	The Duke does greet you, general,	
	And he requires your haste-posthaste appearance	
	Even on the instant.	

| OTHELLO | What is the matter, think you? | |

CASSIO	Something from Cyprus, as I may divine.	
	It is a business of some heat. The galleys	40
	Have sent a dozen sequent messengers	
	This very night at one another's heels –	
	And many of the consuls, raised and met,	
	Are at the Duke's already. You have been hotly called for.	
	When, being not at your lodging to be found,	45
	The Senate hath sent about three several quests	
	To search you out.	

OTHELLO	'Tis well I am found by you.	
	I will but spend a word here in the house,	
	And go with you.	

Exit.

| CASSIO | Ancient, what makes he here? | |

| IAGO | Faith, he tonight hath boarded a land carrack. | 50 |
| | If it prove lawful prize, he's made forever. | |

| CASSIO | I do not understand. | |

| IAGO | He's married. | |

| CASSIO | To who? | |

Re-enter OTHELLO.

| IAGO | Marry, to – Come, captain, will you go? | |

Brabantio arrives and accuses Othello of having used magic spells to make Desdemona love him. Brabantio unsuccessfully tries to have Othello arrested.

THINK ABOUT for GCSE

Characterisation
- Why does Iago single out Roderigo as his opponent in line 58 when it looks as though a fight might break out?

Themes and issues
- **Race**: Like Iago and Roderigo, Brabantio insults Othello because of his black skin. Find the occasions where he (a) links Othello with the devil (believed to be black); (b) refers insultingly to Othello's colour; and (c) assumes that his daughter would have been frightened of Othello's looks.

53 **Have**: I'll go

55 **advised**: careful

58 **I am for you**: I'm your opponent

60 **years**: age

63 **enchanted**: bewitched
64 **I'll refer ... sense**: I ask you use your common sense to judge

67 **opposite to**: against the idea of
68 **curlèd**: curly haired (i.e. pampered)
69 **t' incur ... mock**: to make herself publicly mocked
70 **her guardage**: her father's guardianship
72 **gross in sense**: blatantly obvious
73 **practised ... charms**: put her under disgusting spells
74 **minerals**: i.e. poisons
75 **motion**: the mind
   disputed on: debated
76 **'Tis ... thinking**: it makes sense
77 **apprehend ... attach**: arrest
79 **arts ... warrant**: i.e. black magic

OTHELLO	Have with you.
CASSIO	Here comes another troop to seek for you.

Enter BRABANTIO *with* RODERIGO, *and others with lights and weapons.*

IAGO	It is Brabantio. General, be advised. He comes to bad intent.	55
OTHELLO	Holla! Stand there!	
RODERIGO	Signior, it is the Moor.	
BRABANTIO	Down with him, thief!	

Some, on both sides, draw their swords.

IAGO	You, Roderigo? Come, sir, I am for you.	
OTHELLO	Keep up your bright swords, for the dew will rust them. Good signior, you shall more command with years Than with your weapons.	60
BRABANTIO	O thou foul thief! – Where hast thou stowed my daughter? Damned as thou art, thou hast enchanted her! For I'll refer me to all things of sense, If she in chains of magic were not bound, Whether a maid so tender, fair, and happy, So opposite to marriage that she shunned The wealthy, curlèd darlings of our nation, Would ever have, t' incur a general mock, Run from her guardage to the sooty bosom Of such a thing as thou! – to fear, not to delight! Judge me the world if 'tis not gross in sense That thou hast practised on her with foul charms – Abused her delicate youth with drugs or minerals That weaken motion. I'll have't disputed on – 'Tis probable, and palpable to thinking. I therefore apprehend and do attach thee For an abuser of the world, a practiser Of arts inhibited and out of warrant. (*To the officers*) Lay hold upon him! If he do resist, Subdue him at his peril.	65 70 75 80

Othello and Brabantio set off to see the Duke.

82 of my inclining: on my side

86 course ... session: i.e. the next sitting of the court

90 present: urgent / immediate

95 idle cause: unimportant case

98 have passage free: be allowed
99 pagans: non-Christians

THINK ABOUT *for* GCSE

Language

- Shakespeare often uses imagery of the theatre and acting. What effect does this have in lines 83 to 84?

Themes and issues

- **Race**: Look at lines 76 to 79 and 98 to 99. What is Brabantio suggesting here about the ways Othello's background and origins have supposedly affected his behaviour?

OTHELLO	Hold your hands – Both you of my inclining and the rest. Were it my cue to fight, I should have known it Without a prompter. Whither will you that I go To answer this your charge?
BRABANTIO	To prison, till fit time Of law and course of direct session Call thee to answer.
OTHELLO	What if I do obey? How may the Duke be therewith satisfied, Whose messengers are here about my side Upon some present business of the state To bring me to him?
OFFICER	'Tis true, most worthy signior. The Duke's in council, and your noble self I am sure is sent for.
BRABANTIO	How? The Duke in council? In this time of the night? – Bring him away. Mine's not an idle cause. The Duke himself, Or any of my brothers of the state, Cannot but feel this wrong as 'twere their own: For if such actions may have passage free, Bondslaves and pagans shall our statesmen be.

85

90

95

Exeunt.

In this scene ...

- The Duke and senators have received reports that a fleet of Turkish ships is heading towards Cyprus.
- Othello explains how he won Desdemona's love, but Brabantio is still unhappy about the marriage.
- Othello is put in charge of the defence of Cyprus. The Duke agrees that Desdemona can go with him.
- Iago persuades Roderigo to follow Othello and Desdemona to Cyprus.

The Duke and senators talk about reports of a fleet of invading Turkish ships.

1   **composition**: consistency
2   **gives them credit**: makes the news believable
   disproportioned: inconsistent

5   **jump not**: do not agree
   just accompt: exact number
6   **aim**: estimate

9   **to judgement**: when you consider it carefully
10 **do ... error**: i.e. am not going to reject the main fact just because the figures are inconsistent
11–12 **approve ... sense**: believe to be a cause for alarm

THINK ABOUT *for* **GCSE**

Structure and form
- How do the structure and language at the opening of this scene convey a sense of urgency and anxiety?

Performance and staging
- How could this opening be staged so as to emphasise the urgency? Think about actors' movements and the way they deliver the lines.

17 **How ... change?**: What do you make of this different report?
18 **assay**: test
   pageant: show / deception
19 **keep ... gaze**: distract us

22 **more concerns**: is more important to

30

Venice: a council-room.

Enter the DUKE *and* SENATORS, *with* OFFICERS, *taking seats at the council-table. Attendants bring lights.*

DUKE	There is no composition in these news That gives them credit.
SENATOR 1	Indeed, they are disproportioned. My letters say a hundred and seven galleys.
DUKE	And mine a hundred and forty.
SENATOR 2	And mine two hundred.

But though they jump not on a just accompt –   5
As in these cases where the aim reports
'Tis oft with difference – yet do they all confirm
A Turkish fleet, and bearing up to Cyprus.

DUKE   Nay, it is possible enough to judgement.
I do not so secure me in the error,   10
But the main article I do approve
In fearful sense.

SAILOR   (*Calling from outide*) What ho! What ho! What ho!

Enter SAILOR.

OFFICER   A messenger from the galleys.

DUKE   Now, what's the business?

SAILOR   The Turkish preparation makes for Rhodes.
So was I bid report here to the state   15
By Signior Angelo.

DUKE   How say you by this change?

SENATOR 1   This cannot be,
By no assay of reason. 'Tis a pageant
To keep us in false gaze. When we consider
The importancy of Cyprus to the Turk,   20
And let ourselves again but understand
That as it more concerns the Turk than Rhodes,

New reports confirm that the Turkish fleet is sailing towards Cyprus. Othello and Brabantio arrive. The Duke tells Othello that he will be needed in the war against the Turks.

23 **with … it**: capture it more easily
24 **brace**: state of defence

26 **dressed in**: equipped with
27 **unskilful**: lacking in judgement
28 **latest**: till last
29–30 **Neglecting … profitless**: giving up an easy and profitable undertaking to stir up a risky and fruitless one
31 **in all confidence**: we can be sure

33 **Ottomites**: Turks

35 **injointed**: joined up
after: following

37 **restem**: retrace
38 **backward**: original
frank: open (i.e. no longer disguised)

41 **free duty**: willing service
recommends you thus: gives you this information

46 **post-posthaste dispatch**: send it most urgently

48 **straight**: immediately
49 **general**: universal

51 **counsel**: advice

THINK ABOUT for GCSE

Context

• Venice was constantly under threat from the powerful Ottomans (Turks). Having listened to all the reports, the Duke concludes ''Tis certain then for Cyprus' (line 43). Why does it seem more likely that the Turks are heading for Cyprus than Rhodes? Look at the First Senator's argument in lines 17 to 30 and the Messenger's report in lines 33 to 39.

Language

• How does the Duke's language suggest that he is much more interested in Othello's arrival than Brabantio's?

So may he with more facile question bear it,
For that it stands not in such warlike brace,
But altogether lacks th' abilities   **25**
That Rhodes is dressed in. If we make thought of this,
We must not think the Turk is so unskilful
To leave that latest which concerns him first,
Neglecting an attempt of ease and gain
To wake and wage a danger profitless.   **30**

DUKE   Nay, in all confidence he's not for Rhodes.

OFFICER   Here is more news.

    Enter a MESSENGER.

MESSENGER   The Ottomites, reverend and gracious,
Steering with due course toward the isle of Rhodes,
Have there injointed with an after fleet.   **35**

SENATOR 1   Ay, so I thought. How many, as you guess?

MESSENGER   Of thirty sail – and now they do restem
Their backward course, bearing with frank appearance
Their purposes toward Cyprus. Signior Montano,
Your trusty and most valiant servitor,   **40**
With his free duty recommends you thus,
And prays you to believe him.

DUKE   'Tis certain then for Cyprus.
Marcus Luccicos, is not he in town?

SENATOR 1   He's now in Florence.   **45**

DUKE   Write from us to him – post-posthaste dispatch!

SENATOR 1   Here comes Brabantio and the valiant Moor.

    Enter BRABANTIO *and* OTHELLO, *with* CASSIO, IAGO, RODERIGO,
    and Officers.

DUKE   Valiant Othello, we must straight employ you
Against the general enemy Ottoman.
(*To* BRABANTIO) I did not see you. Welcome, gentle
    signior.   **50**
We lacked your counsel and your help tonight.

Brabantio tells the Duke that Othello has used magic to steal Desdemona.

53 **place**: public position (as a senator)
54 **general care**: matters of state
55 **particular**: personal
56 **flood-gate and o'erbearing**: overpowering and overwhelming
57 **engluts**: consumes

61 **mountebanks**: fake doctors
62 **preposterously to err**: make such a ridiculous misjudgement
63 **deficient**: unintelligent
    lame of sense: slow-witted
64 **Sans**: without
66 **beguiled**: deceived / robbed
    herself: i.e. her normal self

69 **After ... sense**: interpreting the law as you see fit
    proper: own
70 **Stood ... action**: faced your charge

72 **mandate**: official orders
73 **hither**: here

THINK ABOUT *for* **GCSE**

Performance and staging

• If you were the director, how would you deal with the number of people on stage from line 48 onwards? Think about the space available on stage and the position of the actors in relation to one another and the audience.

Language

• How does the language at the start of Othello's speech (lines 76 to 81) help the actor to convey a sense of calm, controlled dignity?

---

76 **potent**: powerful
77 **approved**: highly respected

80–1 **The very ... more**: That is the whole extent of my crime
81 **Rude**: Rough

BRABANTIO	So did I yours. Good your Grace, pardon me.
	Neither my place, nor aught I heard of business,
	Hath raised me from my bed; nor doth the general care
	Take hold on me – for my particular grief 55
	Is of so flood-gate and o'erbearing nature
	That it engluts and swallows other sorrows,
	And yet is still itself.
DUKE	Why, what's the matter?
BRABANTIO	My daughter! O, my daughter!
SENATORS	Dead?
BRABANTIO	Ay, to me!
	She is abused, stol'n from me, and corrupted 60
	By spells and medicines bought of mountebanks –
	For nature so preposterously to err,
	Being not deficient, blind, or lame of sense,
	Sans witchcraft could not.
DUKE	Whoe'er he be that in this foul proceeding 65
	Hath thus beguiled your daughter of herself,
	And you of her, the bloody book of law
	You shall yourself read in the bitter letter
	After your own sense – yea, though our proper son
	Stood in your action.
BRABANTIO	Humbly I thank your Grace. 70
	Here is the man – this Moor – whom now, it seems,
	Your special mandate for the state affairs
	Hath hither brought.
ALL	We are very sorry for't.
DUKE	(*To* OTHELLO) What in your own part can you say to this?
BRABANTIO	Nothing, but this is so. 75
OTHELLO	Most potent, grave, and reverend signiors,
	My very noble and approved good masters,
	That I have ta'en away this old man's daughter,
	It is most true – true I have married her.
	The very head and front of my offending 80
	Hath this extent, no more. Rude am I in my speech,

Othello offers to explain to the Duke how he won Desdemona, but Brabantio repeats his accusations.

83 **since ... pith**: i.e. since I was seven
84 **moons wasted**: months ago
85 **the tented field**: battle

87 **pertains to**: has to do with
broil: fighting

90 **round**: blunt

92 **conjuration**: magic spells

95–6 **motion ... herself**: she was shy of her own feelings
97 **credit**: reputation

99 **maimed**: warped
100–1 **so could ... nature**: could act so unnaturally
102 **practices ... hell**: devilish plots
103 **vouch**: claim
104 **blood**: passions / nature
105 **dram ... effect**: magic potion created for this purpose
106 **wrought**: worked
vouch this: make this accusation
107 **wider**: fuller
overt: obvious
108 **thin habits**: flimsy evidence
109 **modern seeming**: common beliefs
do prefer: are offered as evidence
111 **indirect ... courses**: cunning plots
113–4 **such fair ... affordeth**: the pleasant, intimate conversations that two people have

115 **the Sagittary**: the inn where Desdemona is staying
117 **foul**: i.e. guilty

THINK ABOUT for **GCSE**

Themes and issues
- **Race**: What insults about Othello's colour and behaviour is Brabantio voicing in lines 94 to 106? Where have we heard these insults earlier?
- **Gender**: What does Brabantio's speech (lines 94 to 106) reveal about his knowledge of his daughter? What kind of person does he think she is?

And little blessed with the soft phrase of peace –
For since these arms of mine had seven years' pith
Till now some nine moons wasted, they have used
Their dearest action in the tented field;   85
And little of this great world can I speak
More than pertains to feats of broil and battle –
And therefore little shall I grace my cause
In speaking for myself. Yet, by your gracious patience,
I will a round unvarnished tale deliver   90
Of my whole course of love – what drugs, what charms,
What conjuration, and what mighty magic
(For such proceeding I am charged withal)
I won his daughter.

BRABANTIO   A maiden never bold,
Of spirit so still and quiet that her motion   95
Blushed at herself – and she, in spite of nature,
Of years, of country, credit, everything,
To fall in love with what she feared to look on!
It is a judgement maimed and most imperfect
That will confess perfection so could err   100
Against all rules of nature, and must be driven
To find out practices of cunning hell
Why this should be. I therefore vouch again
That with some mixtures powerful o'er the blood,
Or with some dram, conjured to this effect,   105
He wrought upon her.

DUKE   To vouch this is no proof,
Without more wider and more overt test
Than these thin habits and poor likelihoods
Of modern seeming do prefer against him.

SENATOR 1   But Othello, speak.   110
Did you, by indirect and forcèd courses
Subdue and poison this young maid's affections?
Or came it by request, and such fair question
As soul to soul affordeth?

OTHELLO   I do beseech you,
Send for the lady to the Sagittary   115
And let her speak of me before her father.
If you do find me foul in her report,

37

The Duke sends for Desdemona. As they wait for her to arrive, Othello explains how he and Desdemona fell in love.

121 **Ancient**: Standard-bearer

123 **blood**: passions / nature
124 **justly**: truthfully

128 **Still**: continually

THINK ABOUT *for* **GCSE**

Language
• How does Othello make his past adventures sound exciting? Think about the details he includes and his use of strange, exotic vocabulary.

Characterisation
• Othello earlier claimed 'Rude am I in my speech' (line 81). From your first impressions of him, do you think he is being modest or does he genuinely believe that he is not an effective speaker?

133 **chances**: events
134 **moving ... field**: exciting experiences on sea and land
135 **hair-breadth scapes**: escaping by the skin of my teeth
imminent: threatening
breach: hole made in a fortress wall
137 **redemption thence**: release from slavery
139 **antres**: caves
idle: empty
141 **hint**: cue
process: story
143 **Anthropophagi**: cannibals
145 **seriously incline**: 1 be fascinated; 2 lean forward attentively
146 **still**: always
thence: away
147 **with haste dispatch**: complete quickly
149 **discourse**: story
150 **pliant**: favourable

The trust, the office I do hold of you
Not only take away, but let your sentence
Even fall upon my life.

DUKE   Fetch Desdemona hither.   **120**

OTHELLO   (*To* IAGO) Ancient, conduct them: you best know the
                         place.

Exit IAGO, **with attendants.**

– And till she come, as truly as to heaven
I do confess the vices of my blood,
So justly to your grave ears I'll present
How I did thrive in this fair lady's love,   **125**
And she in mine.

DUKE   Say it, Othello.

OTHELLO   Her father loved me, oft invited me –
Still questioned me the story of my life
From year to year, the battles, sieges, fortunes
That I have passed.   **130**
I ran it through – even from my boyish days
To the very moment that he bade me tell it.
Wherein I spoke of most disastrous chances,
Of moving accidents by flood and field,
Of hair-breadth scapes i' the imminent deadly breach, **135**
Of being taken by the insolent foe
And sold to slavery, of my redemption thence
And with it all my travels' history –
Wherein of antres vast and deserts idle,
Rough quarries, rocks, and hills whose heads touch
     heaven,   **140**
It was my hint to speak. Such was my process –
And of the Cannibals that each other eat,
The Anthropophagi, and men whose heads
Do grow beneath their shoulders. These things to hear
Would Desdemona seriously incline –   **145**
But still the house affairs would draw her thence;
Which ever as she could with haste dispatch,
She'd come again, and with a greedy ear
Devour up my discourse. Which I observing,
Took once a pliant hour, and found good means   **150**

The Duke is satisfied by Othello's account, but Brabantio demands to hear Desdemona's side of the story.

152 **all my pilgrimage dilate**: relate all my travels in detail

153 **by parcels**: in bits and pieces

154 **intentively**: paying continuous attention

155 **did beguile ... tears**: brought her to tears

159 **passing**: exceedingly

162 **heaven ... her**: i.e. she had been born

THINK ABOUT for GCSE

Relationships

• From Othello's account of his wooing (lines 127 to 169), how would you describe his love for Desdemona, and her love for him? What caused each one to fall in love with the other? In what ways did Desdemona encourage him?

Characterisation

• When Desdemona enters, she is in a very difficult position. How far does she succeed in being tactful and sensitive in her first speech (lines 179 to 188), while at the same time expressing herself clearly and directly?

172 **Take up ... best**: make the best of this trouble

176–7 **my bad ... man**: I have accused him wrongly

183 **You ... duty**: I owe you all the respect due to a father

184 **hitherto**: up to this moment

To draw from her a prayer of earnest heart
That I would all my pilgrimage dilate,
Whereof by parcels she had something heard,
But not intentively. I did consent –
And often did beguile her of her tears   155
When I did speak of some distressful stroke
That my youth suffered. My story being done,
She gave me for my pains a world of sighs –
She swore in faith 'twas strange, 'twas passing strange;
'Twas pitiful, 'twas wondrous pitiful.   160
She wished she had not heard it, yet she wished
That heaven had made her such a man. She thanked me,
And bade me, if I had a friend that loved her,
I should but teach him how to tell my story,
And that would woo her. Upon this hint I spake.   165
She loved me for the dangers I had passed,
And I loved her that she did pity them.
This only is the witchcraft I have used.
Here comes the lady. Let her witness it.

Re-enter IAGO, *with attendants, bringing* DESDEMONA.

DUKE   I think this tale would win my daughter too.   170
                   Good Brabantio –
                   Take up this mangled matter at the best:
                   Men do their broken weapons rather use
                   Than their bare hands.

BRABANTIO   I pray you hear her speak.
                   If she confess that she was half the wooer,   175
                   Destruction on my head if my bad blame
                   Light on the man! Come hither, gentle mistress.
                   Do you perceive in all this noble company
                   Where most you owe obedience?

DESDEMONA   My noble father,
                   I do perceive here a divided duty.   180
                   To you I am bound for life and education:
                   My life and education both do learn me
                   How to respect you. You are lord of all my duty:
                   I am hitherto your daughter. But here's my husband.
                   And so much duty as my mother showed   185

41

Desdemona declares that her first duty now lies with her husband rather than her father. The Duke tries unsuccessfully to make Brabantio realise that he must learn to accept this.

187 **challenge**: claim

190 **I had … get it**: I wish I had adopted a child rather than been a natural father

193 **but thou hast**: if you did not have her

197 **clogs**: heavy weights (to stop animals straying)

198 **lay a sentence**: offer you a proverb

199 **grise**: stair

201 **remedies are past**: matters are past repair

202 **late**: recently

203 **mischief**: harm

204 **next**: surest

206 **Patience**: accepting things as they are
     her … makes: helps us to accept hardships easily

207 **robbed**: victim of a robbery

208 **bootless**: fruitless

209 **let … beguile**: let's allow the Turks to cheat us out of Cyprus

211 **sentence**: proverb

212 **comfort**: comforting advice

215–6 **These … equivocal**: These proverbs can be interpreted two ways – with a comforting or a bitter meaning

218 **was … ear**: i.e. could be cured by words

221 **fortitude**: strength of the defences

222 **substitute**: deputy (i.e. Montano, Govenor of Cyprus)

222–3 **of most … sufficiency**: who is known to be very able

223–4 **opinion … effects**: general opinion, a powerful influence

THINK ABOUT for GCSE

Language

- When Desdemona enters, she is in a very difficult position. How far does she succeed in being tactful and sensitive in her first speech (lines 179 to 188), while at the same time expressing herself clearly and directly?

- Look at lines 201 to 218. What effect do the rhyming couplets have during this exchange?

Relationships

- What have you learned so far about Desdemona's relationship with her father Brabantio?

To you, preferring you before her father,
So much I challenge that I may profess
Due to the Moor my lord.

BRABANTIO   God be with you. I have done.
Please it your Grace, on to the state affairs.
I had rather to adopt a child than get it.   190
Come hither, Moor.
I here do give thee that with all my heart
Which, but thou hast already, with all my heart
I would keep from thee. For your sake, jewel,
I am glad at soul I have no other child –   195
For thy escape would teach me tyranny
To hang clogs on them. I have done, my lord.

DUKE   Let me speak like yourself and lay a sentence
Which, as a grise or step, may help these lovers
Into your favour.   200
When remedies are past the griefs are ended
By seeing the worst, which late on hopes depended.
To mourn a mischief that is past and gone
Is the next way to draw new mischief on.
What cannot be preserved when fortune takes,   205
Patience her injury a mockery makes.
The robbed that smiles, steals something from the thief:
He robs himself that spends a bootless grief.

BRABANTIO   So let the Turk of Cyprus us beguile:
We lose it not so long as we can smile.   210
He bears the sentence well that nothing bears
But the free comfort which from thence he hears –
But he bears both the sentence and the sorrow
That to pay grief must of poor patience borrow.
These sentences, to sugar or to gall,   215
Being strong on both sides, are equivocal.
But words are words. I never yet did hear
That the bruisèd heart was piercèd through the ear.
Beseech you now – to the affairs o' the state.

DUKE   The Turk with a most mighty preparation makes for   220
Cyprus. Othello, the fortitude of the place is best known
to you – and though we have there a substitute of most
allowed sufficiency, yet opinion, a more sovereign

Othello is told that the Turks are about to attack Cyprus and that he must take charge of its defence. Desdemona asks to be allowed to go with him.

THINK ABOUT for GCSE

Language

- What effect could the change from rhyming couplets (lines 201 to 218), to prose (lines 220 to 227), then to blank verse (line 228 onwards) have in performance? In what ways does prose suit what the Duke has to say, for example?

Context

- The Venetians employed many soldiers from other countries. Othello is one example of this practice and we are never allowed to forget that he has been a soldier since childhood. What did we learn in lines 83 to 85? What do lines 228 to 233 tell us about his attitude to living in harsh conditions?

224 **safer voice**: i.e. people would feel safer with Othello in charge
225 **slubber**: spoil / smear
226–7 **stubborn … expedition**: harsh and violent speed
228 **tyrant custom**: habit, which forces us to behave in certain ways
230 **thrice-driven … down**: softest feather-bed
agnize: admit to
231 **alacrity**: eagerness
232 **hardness**: a harsh way of life
234 **bending … state**: bowing / submitting to your authority
235 **crave fit disposition**: beg that suitable arrangements be made
236 **Due … place**: appropriate accommodation
exhibition: financial support
237 **besort**: attendants
238 **levels … breeding**: fits her upbringing

243 **my unfolding**: what I have to say
lend … ear: listen favourably
244 **charter**: support
245 **simpleness**: innocence
247 **downright violence**: drastic actions
248 **subdued**: devoted
249 **quality**: inner nature
250 **I saw … mind**: i.e. she loved his character, rather than his face
251 **valiant parts**: soldierly virtues
252 **consecrate**: dedicate
254 **moth**: i.e. an idle creature
255 **The rites … me**: I would be denied the role and loving my marriage should give me
256 **I … support**: i.e. the time will pass very slowly and sadly for me

| | mistress of effects, throws a more safer voice on you. You must therefore be content to slubber the gloss of your new fortunes with this more stubborn and boisterous expedition. | 225 |

OTHELLO The tyrant custom, most grave senators,
Hath made the flinty and steel couch of war
My thrice-driven bed of down. I do agnize   230
A natural and prompt alacrity
I find in hardness, and do undertake
These present wars against the Ottomites.
Most humbly therefore, bending to your state,
I crave fit disposition for my wife,   235
Due reference of place and exhibition –
With such accommodation and besort
As levels with her breeding.

DUKE   If you please,
Be 't at her father's.

BRABANTIO   I'll not have it so.

OTHELLO Nor I.

DESDEMONA   Nor I – I would not there reside   240
To put my father in impatient thoughts
By being in his eye. Most gracious Duke,
To my unfolding lend your prosperous ear,
And let me find a charter in your voice
T' assist my simpleness.

DUKE   What would you, Desdemona?   245

DESDEMONA That I did love the Moor to live with him,
My downright violence and storm of fortunes
May trumpet to the world. My heart's subdued
Even to the very quality of my lord.
I saw Othello's visage in his mind –   250
And to his honours and his valiant parts
Did I my soul and fortunes consecrate.
So that, dear lords, if I be left behind,
A moth of peace, and he go to the war,
The rites for why I love him are bereft me,   255
And I a heavy interim shall support
By his dear absence. Let me go with him.

Othello asks that Desdemona's request to go with him to Cyprus should be granted. The Duke agrees and orders them to leave immediately.

THINK ABOUT for GCSE

Context

- In certain families during Shakespeare's time, a woman could not always choose her husband. How far does that fact help you to understand Desdemona's actions?

- The Duke (or 'Doge') was the Venetian Head of State. In what ways has his power been an important feature of this scene? How has it been used in ways that affect Othello and Desdemona?

Themes and issues

- **Reputation and honour**: Othello describes Iago as a man 'of honesty and trust' (line 282). This is an example of dramatic irony – where we know something that a character does not. What job is Othello giving Iago here, and why are those qualities important for it?

Language

- This part of the scene ends with two more couplets (lines 287 to 288 and 290 to 291). How might the audience react to each one?

258 **voice**: consent
259 **Vouch**: Bear witness
260 **To please … appetite**: for my own pleasure
261 **comply with heat**: to satisfy sexual desire
261–2 **the young … defunct**: the passion I had as a young man which has now died away
263 **free and bounteous**: generous
265 **scant**: neglect
266 **For**: because
266–7 **light-winged … Cupid**: i.e. the light-hearted attractions of love-making
267–8 **seel … instruments**: i.e. make me blind with pleasure and unable to function
269 **That … business**: so that sex gets in the way of my work
270 **skillet**: saucepan
271 **indign … adversities**: unworthy and shameful misfortunes
272 **Make head … estimation**: attack my reputation
273 **determine**: decide

279 **commission**: orders
280 **quality**: importance
     respect: relevance
281 **import**: concern
     ancient: standard-bearer
283 **conveyance**: i.e. Iago will be Desdemona's escort

287 **delighted**: delightful

OTHELLO	Let her have your voice.
	Vouch with me, heaven, I therefore beg it not
	To please the palate of my appetite, 260
	Nor to comply with heat (the young affects
	In me defunct) and proper satisfaction –
	But to be free and bounteous to her mind.
	And heaven defend your good souls that you think
	I will your serious and great business scant 265
	For she is with me. No: when light-winged toys
	Of feathered Cupid seel with wanton dullness
	My speculative and officed instruments,
	That my disports corrupt and taint my business,
	Let housewives make a skillet of my helm – 270
	And all indign and base adversities
	Make head against my estimation!
DUKE	Be it as you shall privately determine,
	Either for her stay or going. Th' affair cries haste,
	And speed must answer it. You must hence tonight. 275
DESDEMONA	Tonight, my lord?
DUKE	This night.
OTHELLO	With all my heart.
DUKE	At nine i' the morning here we'll meet again.
	Othello, leave some officer behind,
	And he shall our commission bring to you,
	With such things else of quality and respect 280
	As doth import you.
OTHELLO	So please your Grace, my ancient:
	A man he is of honesty and trust.
	To his conveyance I assign my wife,
	With what else needful your good Grace shall think
	To be sent after me.
DUKE	Let it be so. 285
	Good night to every one. (*To* BRABANTIO) And, noble signior,
	If virtue no delighted beauty lack,
	Your son-in-law is far more fair than black.
SENATOR 1	Adieu, brave Moor. Use Desdemona well.

Brabantio warns Othello that
if Desdemona is prepared to
deceive her father she may
also deceive her husband.
Othello and Desdemona go to
prepare for departure to Cyprus.
Roderigo threatens to kill
himself for love of Desdemona.

292 **faith**: faithfulness

294 **I prithee**: Please
295 **in ... advantage**: at the earliest
     opportunity
297 **direction**: instructions

THINK ABOUT for GCSE

Language
- What dramatic irony can
  you find when you set the
  first half of line 292 against
  the second half? What is
  the effect of this on the
  audience?

- In Shakespeare's time
  people often used 'thou'
  when speaking to a close
  friend or when speaking to
  inferiors. In Act 1 Scene 1
  Iago addressed Roderigo as
  'you' (the polite form), but
  from here on he uses 'thou'.
  Why has he changed?

303 **incontinently**: immediately

307 **prescription**: 1 right; 2 doctor's order

312 **guinea-hen**: 1 woman; 2 prostitute

315 **fond**: foolishly in love
     virtue: nature
316 **A fig**: i.e. What use is that?
319 **set**: plant
     hyssop ... thyme: herbs
     gender: kind

BRABANTIO	Look to her, Moor, if thou hast eyes to see: 290 She has deceived her father, and may thee.
OTHELLO	My life upon her faith!

> *Exit the* DUKE, *with* BRABANTIO, SENATORS,
    CASSIO, OFFICERS *and attendants.*

	– Honest Iago, My Desdemona must I leave to thee. I prithee let thy wife attend on her, And bring them after in the best advantage. 295 Come, Desdemona, I have but an hour Of love, of worldly matters and direction, To spend with thee. We must obey the time.

> *Exit* OTHELLO, *with* DESDEMONA.

RODERIGO	Iago?
IAGO	What say'st thou, noble heart? 300
RODERIGO	What will I do, think'st thou?
IAGO	Why, go to bed and sleep.
RODERIGO	I will incontinently drown myself.
IAGO	If thou dost, I shall never love thee after. Why, thou silly gentleman? 305
RODERIGO	It is silliness to live when to live is torment – and then have we a prescription to die when death is our physician.
IAGO	O villainous! I have looked upon the world for four times seven years, and since I could distinguish betwixt a benefit and an injury, I never found man that knew 310 how to love himself. Ere I would say I would drown myself for the love of a guinea-hen, I would change my humanity with a baboon.
RODERIGO	What should I do? I confess it is my shame to be so fond, but it is not in my virtue to amend it. 315
IAGO	Virtue? A fig! 'Tis in ourselves that we are thus, or thus. Our bodies are our gardens, to the which our wills are gardeners. So that if we will plant nettles or sow lettuce, set hyssop and weed up thyme, supply it with one gender

Iago talks Roderigo out of killing himself. He argues that Desdemona will soon tire of Othello and persuades him that his best plan is to get money together and follow the couple to Cyprus.

THINK ABOUT for GCSE

Characterisation

• At the beginning of this exchange, Roderigo talks about drowning himself (line 303). What does Iago say to dissuade him (lines 316 to 355)? How does Iago regain Roderigo's confidence and trust?

• Iago advises Roderigo to follow the army to Cyprus, disguising himself with a false beard (lines 335 to 336). What else does Iago keep telling Roderigo to do? What might Iago's plans be, and how might they involve Roderigo?

320 **distract it with**: divide it among
sterile: infertile
321 **manured**: fertilised
322 **corrigible authority**: power to correct
323 **poise**: balance out
326 **conclusions**: behaviour / ends
327 **carnal stings**: sexual desires
unbitted: unbridled / unrestrained
328 **sect**: cutting
scion: shoot

330–1 **permission of the will**: lack of self control
333 **knit ... deserving**: determined to help you get what you deserve
334 **perdurable**: everlasting
stead: help
336 **defeat thy favour**: disguise your appearance
usurped: i.e. false

340–1 **answerable sequestration**: i.e. similar separation from Othello
341 **put but**: just put
344 **locusts**: a sweet fruit
coloquintida: a bitter apple
345 **is sated with**: has had enough of

348 **more delicate**: nicer
349 **sanctimony**: holiness (of marriage)
350 **erring**: 1 wandering; 2 sinful
super-subtle: sophisticated / delicate

353 **clean ... way**: a crazy idea
354 **compassing**: achieving

356 **be fast to**: wholeheartedly support
issue: outcome

of herbs or distract it with many – either to have it sterile 320
with idleness or manured with industry – why, the power
and corrigible authority of this lies in our wills. If the
balance of our lives had not one scale of reason to poise
another of sensuality, the blood and baseness of our
natures would conduct us to most preposterous 325
conclusions. But we have reason to cool our raging
motions, our carnal stings, our unbitted lusts – whereof I
take this that you call love to be a sect or scion.

RODERIGO   It cannot be.

IAGO   It is merely a lust of the blood and a permission of the 330
will. Come, be a man! Drown thyself? Drown cats and
blind puppies! I have professed me thy friend, and I
confess me knit to thy deserving with cables of
perdurable toughness. I could never better stead thee
than now. Put money in thy purse. Follow thou the wars; 335
defeat thy favour with an usurped beard. I say, put
money in thy purse. It cannot be long that Desdemona
should continue her love to the Moor – put money in
thy purse – nor he his to her. It was a violent
commencement, and thou shalt see an answerable 340
sequestration – put but money in thy purse. These
Moors are changeable in their wills – fill thy purse with
money. The food that to him now is as luscious as
locusts shall be to him shortly as bitter as coloquintida.
She must change for youth; when she is sated with his 345
body, she will find the error of her choice. Therefore, put
money in thy purse. If thou wilt needs damn thyself, do
it a more delicate way than drowning. Make all the
money thou canst. If sanctimony and a frail vow betwixt
an erring barbarian and a super-subtle Venetian be not 350
too hard for my wits and all the tribe of hell, thou shalt
enjoy her. Therefore make money! A pox of drowning
thyself! – it is clean out of the way. Seek thou rather to
be hanged in compassing thy joy than to be drowned
and go without her. 355

RODERIGO   Wilt thou be fast to my hopes, if I depend on the issue?

IAGO   Thou art sure of me. Go, make money. I have told thee
often, and I retell thee again and again: I hate the Moor.

Iago expresses his hatred for Othello and plots his revenge.

359 hearted: heart-felt

359–60 be conjunctive: work together

361 cuckold him: make him a man whose wife has been unfaithful

363 Traverse: Quick march!

367 betimes: early

368 Go to: All right then

THINK ABOUT for GCSE

Language
- What does Iago appear to be telling Roderigo in lines 362 to 363? How effective is the image he uses?

Relationships
- How would you describe the relationship between Iago and Roderigo?

Characterisation
- It has been said that in this first soliloquy (lines 374 to 395) we see Iago 'without a mask' for the first time. What do we learn about his secret feelings and the ways he views other people? Think about his attitude to Roderigo, Othello and Cassio, and how they relate to his plan.

374 ever … purse: i.e. always get money out of fools I deceive

375 mine … profane: abuse my own wisdom

376 snipe: fool

378 it … abroad: people say

378–9 'twixt … office: i.e. he has had sex with my wife

381 as if for surety: as though it were a certain fact

holds me well: thinks highly of me

383 proper: handsome

384 place: position (as lieutenant)

plume … will: do exactly what I want

385 double knavery: i.e. injuring both Othello and Cassio

386 abuse … ears: deceive Othello into believing

388 person: appearance

dispose: manner

389 framed: created

false: unfaithful

My cause is hearted: thine hath no less reason. Let us
be conjunctive in our revenge against him. If thou canst   360
cuckold him, thou dost thyself a pleasure, me a sport.
There are many events in the womb of time, which will
be delivered. Traverse – go! – provide thy money! We
will have more of this tomorrow. Adieu.

RODERIGO	Where shall we meet i' the morning?	365
IAGO	At my lodging.	
RODERIGO	I'll be with thee betimes.	
IAGO	Go to, farewell. – Do you hear, Roderigo?	
RODERIGO	What say you?	
IAGO	No more of drowning – do you hear?	370
RODERIGO	I am changed.	
IAGO	Go to – farewell! Put money enough in your purse.	
RODERIGO	I'll sell all my land.	

Exit.

IAGO   Thus do I ever make my fool my purse –
For I mine own gained knowledge should profane   375
If I would time expend with such a snipe
But for my sport and profit. I hate the Moor –
And it is thought abroad that 'twixt my sheets
He's done my office. I know not if 't be true –
Yet I, for mere suspicion in that kind,   380
Will do, as if for surety. He holds me well:
The better shall my purpose work on him.
Cassio's a proper man. Let me see now:
To get his place, and to plume up my will
In double knavery. How? How? Let's see.   385
After some time, to abuse Othello's ears
That he is too familiar with his wife.
He hath a person and a smooth dispose
To be suspected – framed to make women false.
The Moor is of a free and open nature,   390

Iago concludes his soliloquy and vows to put his plan into action.

394 engendered: created / conceived

THINK ABOUT *for* GCSE

Language

- Shakespeare often ends a section or scene with a couplet (a pair of lines that rhyme). What effects can this have? Look at Act 1 Scene 2, lines 98 to 99 and Act 1 Scene 3, lines 394 to 395.

Characterisation

- What does the final couplet reveal about Iago and his plans? What similarities are there with the language of lines 362 to 363?

That thinks men honest that but seem to be so –
And will as tenderly be led by the nose
As asses are.
I have 't! It is engendered! Hell and night
Must bring this monstrous birth to the world's light.   **395**

Exit.

In this scene ...

- The fleet of invading Turkish ships is destroyed in a storm.
- Cassio, Iago and Desdemona arrive safely in Cyprus. Having seen Othello arrive, Iago states his plan to destroy the couple's happiness.
- Iago tells Roderigo that Desdemona and Cassio are in love and explains how Roderigo can help to get Cassio dismissed from his post. Alone, he thinks through his plans to destroy Othello.

On Cyprus, news comes that the fleet of Turkish ships has been destroyed in a storm.

1 **discern**: make out

2 **high-wrought flood**: angry sea
3 **main**: sea
4 **Descry**: make out

7 **ruffianed**: raged

9 **hold the mortise**: keep their joints together
10 **segregation**: scattering

12 **chidden billow**: scolded sea
    pelt: drench

14 **burning Bear**: bright Little Bear constellation
15 **guards**: the two brightest stars in the constellation
    pole: the pole star (essential to navigation)
16 **like molestation**: such an upheaval
17 **enchafèd flood**: enraged sea
18 **embayed**: safe in a bay
19 **bear it out**: survive

22 **designment halts**: battle plan is crippled
23 **sufferance**: damage

THINK ABOUT for GCSE

Structure and form
- How can you tell from the dialogue that the scene has shifted from Venice?

Performance and staging
- If you were the director, how would you stage this scene in a modern theatre? Think about scenery, staging, lighting and sound effects.

Cyprus: above the island's harbour.

Enter Montano (*Governor of Cyprus*), *meeting with two* Gentlemen.

Montano	What from the cape can you discern at sea?
Gentleman 1	Nothing at all! – It is a high-wrought flood. I cannot 'twixt the heaven and the main Descry a sail.
Montano	Methinks the wind hath spoke aloud at land! – 5 A fuller blast ne'er shook our battlements. If it hath ruffianed so upon the sea, What ribs of oak, when mountains melt on them, Can hold the mortise? What shall we hear of this?
Gentleman 2	A segregation of the Turkish fleet – 10 For do but stand upon the foaming shore, The chidden billow seems to pelt the clouds! The wind-shaked surge, with high and monstrous main, Seems to cast water on the burning Bear And quench the guards of th' ever-fixèd pole. 15 I never did like molestation view On the enchafèd flood.
Montano	If that the Turkish fleet Be not ensheltered and embayed, they are drowned! It is impossible they bear it out.

Enter a third Gentleman.

Gentleman 3	News, lads! Our wars are done! 20 The desperate tempest hath so banged the Turks That their designment halts. A noble ship of Venice Hath seen a grievous wreck and sufferance On most part of their fleet.
Montano	How? Is this true?

Cassio arrives. He became separated from Othello in the storm, but is hopeful that he is safe.

25 **put in**: harboured
26 **Veronesa**: a type of Italian ship

29 **is … commission**: has full powers

32 **Touching**: concerning
    sadly: serious / grave

36 **full**: excellent

38 **throw … eyes**: keep watch
39–40 **the main … regard**: the sea and sky become indistinguishable

41–2 **is … arrivance**: we are expecting the arrival of more ships

44 **approve**: honour

48 **bark**: ship
49 **Of … allowance**: with a proven reputation
50–1 **not surfeited … cure**: i.e. I am not over-optimistic but I am confident

53 **brow**: cliff-edge

55 **My hopes … for**: I hope it is

THINK ABOUT for GCSE

Themes and issues
• **Reputation and honour**: What do we learn from the dialogue between Montano and the Gentleman in lines 25 to 42 about Othello's reputation?

Language
• In lines 50 to 51 'surfeited' means 'eaten too much', and 'Stand in bold cure' literally means 'looks healthy'. How does the image help to get across the idea that Cassio's confidence is not simply wild optimism, but based on reason?

GENTLEMAN 3	The ship is here put in – **25** A Veronesa. Michael Cassio, Lieutenant to the warlike Moor Othello, Is come on shore – the Moor himself at sea, And is in full commission here for Cyprus.
MONTANO	I am glad on't. 'Tis a worthy governor. **30**
GENTLEMAN 3	But this same Cassio, though he speak of comfort Touching the Turkish loss, yet he looks sadly And prays the Moor be safe – for they were parted With foul and violent tempest.
MONTANO	Pray heavens he be! – For I have served him, and the man commands **35** Like a full soldier. Let's to the seaside, ho! As well to see the vessel that's come in As to throw out our eyes for brave Othello, Even till we make the main and th' aerial blue An indistinct regard.
GENTLEMAN 3	Come, let's do so – **40** For every minute is expectancy Of more arrivance.

Enter CASSIO.

CASSIO	Thanks, you the valiant of this warlike isle, That so approve the Moor. O, let the heavens Give him defence against their elements! – **45** For I have lost him on a dangerous sea.
MONTANO	Is he well shipped?
CASSIO	His bark is stoutly timbered, and his pilot Of very expert and approved allowance. Therefore my hopes, not surfeited to death, **50** Stand in bold cure.

Shouting is heard in the distance – A sail! A sail, a sail!

CASSIO	– What noise?
GENTLEMAN 1	The town is empty. On the brow o' the sea Stand ranks of people, and they cry 'A sail!'
CASSIO	My hopes do shape him for the governor. **55**

News comes that Desdemona has arrived safely, accompanied by Iago. Cassio tells Montano that Othello is married.

56 shot of courtesy: welcoming salute

62 paragons: surpasses
fame: rumour
63 quirks: flowery poetic descriptions
blazoning pens: writers who praise her
64 th' essential … creation: natural outward beauty
65 tire the ingener: defeat the artist's imagination

69 guttered: jagged
congregated sands: sandbanks
70 ensteeped: submerged / underwater
clog … keel: wreck innocent ships
71–2 omit … natures: forget their deadly nature

76–7 Whose … speed: who has arrived a week earlier than expected

81 extincted: dampened

THINK ABOUT *for* GCSE

Language
- What does Cassio's language here tell us about his views of Othello and Desdemona? What does it tell us about Cassio himself?

Structure and form
- How does Shakespeare keep up the tension and suspense about whether Othello will arrive safely throughout the opening of this scene?

A cannon-shot is heard.

GENTLEMAN 2   They do discharge the shot of courtesy –
Our friends at least!

CASSIO   I pray you, sir, go forth
And give us truth who 'tis that is arrived.

GENTLEMAN 2   I shall.

Exit.

MONTANO   But, good lieutenant, is your general wived?   60

CASSIO   Most fortunately. He hath achieved a maid
That paragons description and wild fame –
One that excels the quirks of blazoning pens,
And in th' essential vesture of creation
Does tire the ingener.

Re-enter second GENTLEMAN.

                              – How now? Who has put in?   65

GENTLEMAN 2   'Tis one Iago, ancient to the general.

CASSIO   He's had most favourable and happy speed:
Tempests themselves, high seas, and howling winds,
The guttered rocks and congregated sands,
Traitors ensteeped to clog the guiltless keel,   70
As having sense of beauty, do omit
Their mortal natures, letting go safely by
The divine Desdemona.

MONTANO   What is she?

CASSIO   She that I spake of, our great captain's captain,
Left in the conduct of the bold Iago,   75
Whose footing here anticipates our thoughts
A sevennight's speed. Great Jove, Othello guard!
And swell his sail with Thine own powerful breath –
That he may bless this bay with his tall ship,
Make love's quick pants in Desdemona's arms,   80
Give renewed fire to our extinct spirits,
And bring all Cyprus comfort.

Cassio greets Desdemona and
Emilia, Iago's wife .

84 **let ... knees**: kneel to her

87 **Enwheel thee round**: surround you

89–90 **nor know ... that**: but as far as I am
aware

92 **contention of**: war between
93 **Parted our fellowship**: separated our
ships

THINK ABOUT for GCSE

Characterisation
• When Desdemona enters
(lines 82 to 87), what do
Cassio's language and
behaviour tell us about him?

Performance and staging
• Cassio asks Iago not to let
his manner 'gall' Iago's
'patience' (line 97). How
might Cassio's behaviour,
here and earlier, irritate
Iago? How might both
Cassio's behaviour and
Iago's reactions be shown
in performance?

97 **gall your patience**: irritate you
98 **extend my manners**: i.e. by greeting
Emilia with a kiss
breeding: upbringing
99 **gives ... courtesy**: has trained me to
welcome women in such a forward
way
101 **tongue**: talk
bestows on: gives
102 **has no speech**: i.e. doesn't nag you
104 **still**: always
have list: want to

Enter Desdemona, Iago, Roderigo, *and* Emilia.

                                O, behold!
The riches of the ship is come on shore!
You men of Cyprus, let her have your knees.
(*Kneeling*) Hail to thee, lady! – and the grace of heaven,   **85**
Before, behind thee, and on every hand,
Enwheel thee round!

DESDEMONA   I thank you, valiant Cassio.
What tidings can you tell me of my lord?

CASSIO   He is not yet arrived, nor know I aught
But that he's well and will be shortly here.   **90**

DESDEMONA   O – but I fear! How lost you company?

CASSIO   The great contention of sea and skies
Parted our fellowship.

Shouts in the distance again – A sail! A sail! – *and another*
cannon-shot.

                          – But hark – a sail!

GENTLEMAN 2   They give this greeting to the citadel –
This likewise is a friend.

CASSIO   See for the news.   **95**

                      Exit second GENTLEMAN.

(*To* IAGO) Good ancient, you are welcome.
    (*To* EMILIA) Welcome, mistress.
Let it not gall your patience, good Iago,
That I extend my manners. 'Tis my breeding
That gives me this bold show of courtesy.

He kisses EMILIA.

IAGO   Sir, would she give you so much of her lips   **100**
As of her tongue she oft bestows on me,
You would have enough.

DESDEMONA   Alas, she has no speech!

IAGO   In faith, too much.
I find it still when I have list to sleep.

Othello has not yet arrived. To hide her anxiety, Desdemona talks jokingly with Iago.

105 **Marry**: By the Virgin Mary
106–7 **She … thinking**: she keeps quiet sometimes but then nags inwardly

108 **pictures**: i.e. pretty and silent
       bells: i.e. noisy
109–10 **saints … injuries**: look innocent and saintly when you claim to be injured
110–11 **players … housewifery**: spendthrifts or gamblers in your house-keeping
111 **housewives … beds**: mean in bed
112 **fie upon thee**: shame on you

THINK ABOUT for GCSE

Performance and staging
- If you were the director, would you encourage Iago to say the comments about Emilia and women in lines 100 to 114 seriously or in jest? What effect would each way of playing the lines have?

Language
- What image does Iago use in lines 125 to 126 to describe the difficulty of creating a witty comment? How does this compare with the image he used to conclude his soliloquy at the end of Act 1 (Act 1 Scene 3, lines 394 to 395)?

117 **put me to't**: make me try

119 **assay**: give it a try

120–1 **beguile … otherwise**: i.e. am pretending to appear unworried

123 **invention**: inspiration
124 **pate**: head / brain
       bird-lime … frieze: glue from woollen cloth (i.e. with great difficulty)
125 **muse labours**: inspiration is struggling
125–6 **thus … delivered**: this is what it has produced
129 **black**: dark-haired

131 **white**: play on 'wight' (1 man; 2 lover)

	Marry, before your ladyship, I grant	105
	She puts her tongue a *little* in her heart –	
	And chides with thinking.	

EMILIA   You have *little* cause to say so.

IAGO   Come on, come on! You are pictures out of doors, bells
in your parlours, wildcats in your kitchens, saints in
your injuries, devils being offended – players in your   110
housewifery, and housewives in your beds.

DESDEMONA   O, fie upon thee, slanderer!

IAGO   Nay, it is true, or else I am a Turk:
You rise to play, and go to bed to work.

EMILIA   You shall not write *my* praise.

IAGO   No, let me not.   115

DESDEMONA   What wouldst thou write of me, if thou shouldst praise
me?

IAGO   O gentle lady, do not put me to't –
For I am nothing if not critical.

DESDEMONA   Come on, assay. – There's one gone to the harbour?

IAGO   Ay, madam.

DESDEMONA   I am not merry – but I do beguile   120
The thing I am by seeming otherwise.
– Come, how wouldst thou praise me?

IAGO   I am about it: but indeed my invention comes from my
pate as bird-lime does from frieze – it plucks out brains
and all. But my muse labours – and thus she is   125
delivered:
If she be fair and wise: fairness and wit –
The one's for use, the other useth it.

DESDEMONA   Well praised. How if she be black and witty?

IAGO   If she be black, and thereto have a wit,   130
She'll find a white that shall her blackness fit.

DESDEMONA   Worse and worse!

EMILIA   How if fair and foolish?

Iago entertains Desdemona with some rhyming comments about women. When Cassio talks separately to Desdemona, Iago privately comments on Cassio's behaviour towards her.

134 **folly**: sexual irresponsibility

135 **fond paradoxes**: foolish sayings

137 **foul**: ugly

138 **thereunto**: as well

139 **foul pranks**: immoral acts

142 **in the ... merit**: known to be a good woman

143 **put on ... itself**: make even spiteful people praise her

145 **Had ... will**: 1 spoke when she wanted to; 2 was never lost for words

146 **gay**: expensively dressed

147 **Fled ... wish**: did not simply do what she wanted

149 **Bade ... fly**: i.e. accepted injuries done to her and refused to get angry

151 **change ... tail**: i.e. swap a treasure for something worthless

154 **wight**: person

156 **chronicle small beer**: be concerned with unimportant matters

157 **impotent**: weak

159 **profane**: sexually coarse
     liberal: rude

160 **home**: bluntly
     relish ... in: appreciate him more in the character of

162 **well said**: well done

164 **gyve**: shackle / trap

165 **courtship**: courtly manners

THINK ABOUT for GCSE

Themes and issues

• **Gender**: If we take Iago's comments in lines 108 to 156 seriously, what can we say about his view of women? How serious do you think he is?

Structure and form

• In this part of the play Shakespeare once again varies the dialogue, switching from blank verse to rhyming couplets to prose. Think about what effect this has and how the three forms suit what the characters are saying.

| IAGO | She never yet was foolish that was fair – |
| | For even her folly helped her to an heir. |

DESDEMONA	These are old fond paradoxes to make fools laugh i' the 135
	alehouse. What miserable praise hast thou for her that's
	foul and foolish?

| IAGO | There's none so foul, and foolish thereunto, |
| | But does foul pranks which fair and wise ones do. |

DESDEMONA	O heavy ignorance! Thou praisest the worst best. But 140
	what praise couldst thou bestow on a deserving woman
	indeed – one that in the authority of her merit did justly
	put on the vouch of very malice itself?

IAGO	She that was ever fair, and never proud,
	Had tongue at will, and yet was never loud; 145
	Never lacked gold, and yet went never gay,
	Fled from her wish, and yet said 'Now I may' –
	She that being angered, her revenge being nigh,
	Bade her wrong stay, and her displeasure fly –
	She that in wisdom never was so frail 150
	To change the cod's head for the salmon's tail –
	She that could think and ne'er disclose her mind,
	See suitors following, and not look behind:
	She was a wight (if ever such wight were) –

| DESDEMONA | To do what? 155 |

| IAGO | To suckle fools and chronicle small beer. |

DESDEMONA	O most lame and impotent conclusion! Do not learn of
	him, Emilia, though he be thy husband. How say you,
	Cassio? Is he not a most profane and liberal counsellor?

| CASSIO | He speaks home, madam. You may relish him more in 160 |
| | the soldier than in the scholar. |

CASSIO *and* DESDEMONA *talk together.*

IAGO	(*Aside*) He takes her by the palm. Ay, well said –
	whisper! With as little a web as this will I ensnare as
	great a fly as Cassio. Ay – smile upon her, do! I will gyve
	thee in thine own courtship. – 'You say true: 'tis so, 165
	indeed!' – If such tricks as these strip you out of your
	lieutenantry, it had been better you had not kissed your

Othello arrives and expresses his love for Desdemona.

168–9 are most ... in: like to do, playing the fine gentleman

171 clyster-pipes: syringes for injecting medicines into the rectum or vagina

180 labouring bark: struggling ship

181 Olympus: the mountain home of the gods

186 Succeeds ... fate: can be repeated, whatever happens

188 Amen ... powers: May the gods agree

THINK ABOUT for GCSE

Performance and staging

• What do Iago's comments (lines 162 to 171) tell us about the actions that the actor playing Cassio is supposed to perform?

Language

• Find the dramatic irony in Othello's speech (lines 176 to 186). What effect does it have?

• How does the language of music in lines 191 to 193 help to get across both Othello's joy and Iago's plan to destroy it?

three fingers so oft – which now again you are most apt
to play the sir in. Very good! Well kissed! An excellent
courtesy! 'Tis so, indeed. Yet again your fingers to your   170
lips? Would they were clyster-pipes for your sake!

A trumpet-call is heard.

    – The Moor! I know his trumpet.

Cᴀssɪᴏ   'Tis truly so.

Dᴇsᴅᴇᴍᴏɴᴀ   Let's meet him and receive him.

Cᴀssɪᴏ   Lo, where he comes!

Enter Oᴛʜᴇʟʟᴏ, with attendants.

Oᴛʜᴇʟʟᴏ   O my fair warrior!

Dᴇsᴅᴇᴍᴏɴᴀ   My dear Othello!   175

Oᴛʜᴇʟʟᴏ   It gives me wonder great as my content
To see you here before me. O my soul's joy! –
If after every tempest come such calms,
May the winds blow till they have wakened death,
And let the labouring bark climb hills of seas   180
Olympus-high, and duck again as low
As hell's from heaven! If it were now to die,
'Twere now to be most happy – for I fear
My soul hath her content so absolute
That not another comfort like to this   185
Succeeds in unknown fate.

Dᴇsᴅᴇᴍᴏɴᴀ   The heavens forbid
But that our loves and comforts should increase
Even as our days do grow!

Oᴛʜᴇʟʟᴏ   Amen to that, sweet powers!
I cannot speak enough of this content.
It stops me, here (*gesturing to his heart*) – it is too
   much of joy.   190
And this, and this, (*embracing and kissing* Dᴇsᴅᴇᴍᴏɴᴀ)
   the greatest discords be
That e'er our hearts shall make!

Othello and Desdemona go into the fortress. Iago plots to ruin Othello and Desdemona's happiness. He makes Roderigo believe that Desdemona has become tired of Othello and is in love with Cassio.

THINK ABOUT for GCSE

Themes and issues

- **Truth and deception**:
  What do you think Iago means by 'As honest as I am' (line 194)?

Characterisation

- Which instruction of Othello's here might Iago find particularly hurtful? Why?

- Roderigo has been watching Desdemona and Cassio together. Why might he believe Iago's claim that Desdemona is 'directly in love' with Cassio (line 212)? Look back at lines 82 to 87 and 162 to 171.

---

193 set down the pegs: slacken the strings (to make the music out of tune)

196 acquaintance: friends
197 desired: liked

199 prattle ... fashion: chatter irrelevantly
       dote: am foolishly happy
200 comforts: happiness
201 disembark my coffers: have my trunks unloaded
202 master: ship's captain
       citadel: fortress
204 challenge: deserve

207 presently: immediately / soon

210 list: listen to
210–11 watches ... guard: is on guard duty
212 directly: definitely
215 Mark me: Notice / Remember
216 but: only
217 prating: chattering
220 blood: passion
       the act of sport: i.e. sex
221 give ... appetite: freshen the appetite after her desires have been fully satisfied
222 favour: appearance
       sympathy in years: similarity in age
224 required conveniences: necessary conditions
225–6 heave the gorge: retch
226 disrelish: lose the taste for
       abhor: hate

IAGO	(*Aside*) O, you are well tuned now! –
	But I'll set down the pegs that make this music,
	As honest as I am.
OTHELLO	Come, let us to the castle.
	News, friends! Our wars are done: the Turks are
	drowned. 195
	How does my old acquaintance of this isle?
	Honey, you shall be well desired in Cyprus –
	I have found great love amongst them. O my sweet! –
	I prattle out of fashion, and I dote
	In mine own comforts. I prithee, good Iago, 200
	Go to the bay and disembark my coffers.
	Bring thou the master to the citadel –
	He is a good one, and his worthiness
	Does challenge much respect. Come, Desdemona,
	Once more well met at Cyprus! 205

Exit OTHELLO, *with* DESDEMONA, *and all except* IAGO *and*
RODERIGO.

IAGO	(*To an attendant leaving with the others*) Do thou meet
	me presently at the harbour. (*To* RODERIGO) Come hither.
	If thou be'st valiant – as they say base men being in love
	have then a nobility in their natures more than is native
	to them – list me. The lieutenant tonight watches on the 210
	court of guard. First, I must tell thee this: Desdemona is
	directly in love with him.
RODERIGO	With him? Why – 'tis not possible!
IAGO	Lay thy finger thus (*putting his finger to his lips*) and let
	thy soul be instructed. Mark me with what violence she 215
	first loved the Moor but for bragging and telling her
	fantastical lies. And will she love him still for prating? Let
	not thy discreet heart think it. Her eye must be fed. And
	what delight shall she have to look on the devil? When
	the blood is made dull with the act of sport, there should 220
	be – again to inflame it and to give satiety a fresh appetite
	– loveliness in favour, sympathy in years, manners, and
	beauties – all which the Moor is defective in. Now for
	want of these required conveniences, her delicate
	tenderness will find itself abused, begin to heave the 225
	gorge, disrelish and abhor the Moor. Very nature will

Iago instructs Roderigo to pick a fight with Cassio later that night so that Iago can stir up a riot. Because Cassio is in charge of guard duty, he will lose his job.

228–9 pregnant … position: convincing, obvious argument

229 eminent: highly placed

230 voluble: smooth-talking

231 conscionable: conscientious

232 humane seeming: polite manners

compass: achievement

233 salt: lustful

loose affections: immoral desires

234 slipper: slippery

subtle: cunning

finder of occasions: opportunist

235 stamp … advantages: create openings for himself

238 requisites: necessary qualities

green minds: immature / inexperienced people

239 pestilent: detestable / poisonous

239–40 hath found him: 1 has her eye on him; 2 knows what he's after

242 condition: character

245–6 paddle with: fondle

248 index … prologue: contents page and secretive introduction

251 mutualities: intimacies between two people

marshal: show

252 hard at hand: right behind

253 incorporate conclusion: i.e. sex

258 tainting his discipline: sneering at his ability as a soldier

259 minister: provide

261 sudden in choler: quick-tempered

haply: perhaps

263–4 whose … again: i.e. who will not be calmed down again

THINK ABOUT for GCSE

Themes and issues

• **Truth and deception**: From what you have seen of Cassio so far, and bearing in mind that Othello has given him the trusted role of lieutenant, which of the things Iago says about Cassio are likely to be lies, and which might have a basis in truth? Look at lines 228 to 240 and 261 to 262.

Structure and form

• Look at Iago's instructions to Roderigo (lines 254 to 259). What exactly is Iago's plot and what has to happen for it to succeed? How far does it depend on luck?

instruct her in it and compel her to some second choice.
Now sir, this granted – as it is a most pregnant and
unforced position – who stands so eminent in the degree
of this fortune as Cassio does? A knave very voluble – no   230
further conscionable than in putting on the mere form of
civil and humane seeming for the better compass of his
salt and most hidden loose affections. Why, none – why,
none! A slipper and subtle knave, a finder of occasions
– that has an eye can stamp and counterfeit advantages,   235
though true advantage never present itself. A devilish
knave! Besides, the knave is handsome, young, and hath
all those requisites in him that folly and green minds look
after. A pestilent complete knave – and the woman hath
found him already!   240

Roderigo   I cannot believe that in her. She's full of most blessed
condition.

Iago   Blessed fig's-end! The wine she drinks is made of grapes.
If she had been blessed, she would never have loved the
Moor. Blessed pudding! Didst thou not see her paddle   245
with the palm of his hand? Didst not mark that?

Roderigo   Yes, that I did – but that was but courtesy.

Iago   Lechery, by this hand! An index and obscure prologue to
the history of lust and foul thoughts. They met so near with
their lips that their breaths embraced together. Villainous   250
thoughts, Roderigo! When these mutualities so marshal
the way, hard at hand comes the master and main
exercise, the incorporate conclusion. Pish! But, sir, be you
ruled by me. I have brought you from Venice. Watch you
tonight. For the command, I'll lay it upon you. Cassio   255
knows you not. I'll not be far from you. Do you find some
occasion to anger Cassio, either by speaking too loud, or
tainting his discipline – or from what other course you
please which the time shall more favourably minister.

Roderigo   Well. –   260

Iago   Sir, he's rash and very sudden in choler, and haply may
strike at you. Provoke him that he may. For even out of
that will I cause these of Cyprus to mutiny – whose
qualification shall come into no true taste again but by

Roderigo agrees to take part in Iago's plot. Iago gives further reasons for hating Othello and thinks through his plan to destroy him with jealousy.

THINK ABOUT *for* GCSE

Performance and staging

* If you were acting the part of Iago, how would you say 'I must fetch his necessaries ashore' (lines 271 to 272) and why?

Characterisation

* Look at Iago's second soliloquy (lines 274 to 300). List the motives he gives for plotting against Othello and Cassio. How different are they from the motives expressed in his first soliloquy (Act 1 Scene 3, lines 374 to 395)? How far do you think he believes the suspicions he mentions concerning his wife?

* Some people believe that Iago is a skilled plotter who has every detail worked out from the beginning. Others argue that he has only a sketchy outline and is prepared to improvise. Find evidence to support both possibilities. Which one convinces you more, and why?

267 **prefer**: help / promote
   impediment: obstacle
269 **prosperity**: success

271 **warrant**: assure
   by and by: very soon

275 **apt**: likely
   of great credit: very believable
276 **howbeit … not**: even though I can't stand him

280 **out of absolute**: purely out of
   peradventure: perhaps
281 **stand accountant**: could be charged with
282 **diet**: feed
284 **leaped … seat**: i.e. had sex with my wife
285 **inwards**: insides

290 **judgement**: rational thinking
291–2 **trace … hunting**: keep on a leash, because of his hot pursuit (of Desdemona)
292 **stand the putting on**: do what I encourage him to do
293 **on the hip**: at my mercy
294 **Abuse … garb**: tell Othello foul lies about Cassio
295 **with my nightcap**: i.e. has had sex with my wife
297 **egregiously an**: an outstanding
298 **practising upon**: plotting against

| | the displanting of Cassio. So shall you have a shorter | 265 |

the displanting of Cassio. So shall you have a shorter 265
journey to your desires by the means I shall then have
to prefer them – and the impediment most profitably
removed without the which there were no expectation
of our prosperity.

RODERIGO   I will do this if you can bring it to any opportunity.   270

IAGO   I warrant thee. Meet me by and by at the citadel. I must
fetch his necessaries ashore. Farewell.

RODERIGO   Adieu.

Exit.

IAGO   That Cassio loves her, I do well believe it:
That she loves him, 'tis apt and of great credit.   275
The Moor, howbeit that I endure him not,
Is of a constant, loving, noble nature,
And I dare think he'll prove to Desdemona
A most dear husband. Now I do love her too –
Not out of absolute lust, though peradventure   280
I stand accountant for as great a sin,
But partly led to diet my revenge –
For that I do suspect the lusty Moor
Hath leaped into *my* seat – the thought whereof
Doth, like a poisonous mineral, gnaw my inwards.   285
And nothing can or shall content my soul
Till I am evened with him, wife for wife –
Or failing so, yet that I put the Moor
At least into a jealousy so strong
That judgement cannot cure. Which thing to do –   290
If this poor trash of Venice, whom I trace
For his quick hunting, stand the putting on –
I'll have our Michael Cassio on the hip,
Abuse him to the Moor in the rank garb
(For I fear Cassio with my nightcap too),   295
Make the Moor thank me, love me, and reward me
For making him egregiously an ass –
And practising upon his peace and quiet,
Even to madness. 'Tis here (***tapping his head***) – but yet
confused:
Knavery's plain face is never seen till used.   300

Exit.

In this scene ...

- A herald announces the festivities that evening to celebrate the destruction of the Turkish fleet and the marriage of Othello and Desdemona.

2 **certain tidings**: reliable reports
3 **mere perdition**: total loss
4 **triumph**: public celebrations

6 **addiction**: preference / inclination
7 **nuptial**: marriage
8 **offices**: places for getting food and drink
10 **told**: struck

THINK ABOUT
for **GCSE**

Structure and form
- What are the functions of this scene? Why is it important, for example, to let us know that the island is celebrating and that, in particular, 'All offices are open' (line 8)?

Performance and staging
- If you were directing (a) a film, and (b) a stage play of *Othello*, how would you make this scene look and sound exciting?

Cyprus: a street below the fortress.

Enter Othello's Herald, *who reads a proclamation.*

Herald   It is Othello's pleasure, our noble and valiant general,
that upon certain tidings now arrived importing the
mere perdition of the Turkish fleet, every man put
himself into triumph – some to dance, some to make
bonfires, each man to what sport and revels his   5
addiction leads him. For, besides these beneficial news,
it is the celebration of his nuptial. So much was his
pleasure should be proclaimed. All offices are open,
and there is full liberty of feasting from this present
hour of five till the bell have told eleven. Heaven bless   10
the isle of Cyprus and our noble general Othello!

Exit.

In this scene ...

- Iago gets Cassio drunk. A fight breaks out and Cassio wounds Montano.
- Othello dismisses Cassio from his post as lieutenant.
- Iago convinces Cassio that Desdemona can help him get his post back. Iago secretly thinks that if Desdemona pleads on Cassio's behalf, it will help to persuade Othello that she is having an affair with Cassio.

Othello puts Cassio in charge of guard duty. Iago talks to Cassio about Desdemona.

1 **look you to**: take charge of
2 **stop**: self-control / restraint
3 **out-sport discretion**: celebrate too much

6 **honest**: reliable

9 **fruits ... ensue**: enjoyment is ahead

THINK ABOUT for GCSE

Language
- How would you describe the language that Iago uses here to describe Desdemona? What is he suggesting about Desdemona in expressions such as 'sport for Jove' (line 16), 'full of game' (line 18), 'What an eye ... parley to provocation!' (lines 20 to 21) and 'an alarum to love' (line 23)?

Characterisation
- How does Cassio respond to Iago's language? What do his responses reveal about him?

13 **Not this hour**: Not for an hour yet
14 **cast**: dismissed
15–16 **made ... night**: i.e. enjoyed sex
16 **sport for Jove**: i.e. a sexual companion fit for the king of the gods

18 **full of game**: i.e. good in bed

20–1 **sounds ... provocation**: i.e. encourages lustful thoughts

22 **right modest**: very chaste

23 **alarum**: call to arms

Cyprus: inside the fortress.

Enter OTHELLO *and* DESDEMONA, *with* CASSIO *and attendants.*

OTHELLO	Good Michael, look you to the guard tonight.
	Let's teach ourselves that honourable stop,
	Not to out-sport discretion.

CASSIO Iago hath direction what to do –
But notwithstanding, with my personal eye   5
Will I look to't.

OTHELLO   Iago is most honest.
Michael, good night. Tomorrow with your earliest
Let me have speech with you. (*To* DESDEMONA) Come,
        my dear love,
The purchase made, the fruits are to ensue –
That profit's yet to come 'tween me and you.   10
(*To* CASSIO) Good night.

Exit OTHELLO, *with* DESDEMONA *and attendants.*

Enter IAGO.

CASSIO Welcome, Iago. We must to the watch.

IAGO Not this hour, lieutenant: 'tis not yet ten o' the clock. Our
general cast us thus early for the love of his Desdemona
– who let us not therefore blame. He hath not yet made   15
wanton the night with her, and she is sport for Jove.

CASSIO She's a most exquisite lady.

IAGO And, I'll warrant her, full of game.

CASSIO Indeed, she is a most fresh and delicate creature.

IAGO What an eye she has! Methinks it sounds a parley to   20
provocation.

CASSIO An inviting eye – and yet methinks right modest.

IAGO And when she speaks, is it not an alarum to love?

CASSIO She is indeed perfection.

Iago tries to persuade Cassio to
have a drink, knowing that he
gets drunk very easily.

26 **stoup**: jug
    without: outside
    brace: pair
27 **gallants**: young gentlemen
    fain ... measure: gladly drink a toast

32 **I'll drink for you**: i.e. After that I'll
    drink your share

34 **qualified**: diluted / mixed with water
    innovation: disturbance

40 **it dislikes me**: I don't like it

43 **offence**: readiness to take offence

THINK ABOUT _for_ **GCSE**

Characterisation
• What skills does Iago
  display when persuading
  the reluctant Cassio to have
  a drink (lines 12 to 40)?

Structure and form
• What are the functions of
  Iago's aside (lines 41 to 56)?
  Think about what we learn
  about Iago's plot and his
  attitudes to other people.

46–7 **caroused ... pottle-deep**: drunk toasts
      to the bottom of the tankard
47 **watch**: be part of the guard on duty
48 **else**: others
    swelling: arrogant
49 **hold ... distance**: i.e. are quick to take
    offence at any suspected insult to their
    honour
50 **the very elements**: typical of the types
51 **flustered**: confused
54 **offend**: cause trouble in

55 **consequence ... dream**: the outcome
    is what I hope for

IAGO	Well, happiness to their sheets! Come, lieutenant, I **25**
	have a stoup of wine, and here without are a brace of
	Cyprus gallants that would fain have a measure to the
	health of black Othello.
CASSIO	Not tonight, good Iago. I have very poor and unhappy
	brains for drinking. I could well wish courtesy would **30**
	invent some other custom of entertainment.
IAGO	O, they are our friends. But one cup! I'll drink for you.
CASSIO	I have drunk but one cup tonight, and that was craftily
	qualified too – and behold what innovation it makes
	here (**tapping his head**). I am unfortunate in the infirmity **35**
	and dare not task my weakness with any more.
IAGO	What, man! 'Tis a night of revels. The gallants desire it.
CASSIO	Where are they?
IAGO	Here, at the door. I pray you call them in.
CASSIO	I'll do it, but it dislikes me. **40**

Exit.

IAGO	If I can fasten but one cup upon him,
	With that which he hath drunk tonight already,
	He'll be as full of quarrel and offence
	As my young mistress' dog. Now, my sick fool Roderigo,
	Whom love hath turned almost the wrong side out, **45**
	To Desdemona hath tonight caroused
	Potations pottle-deep – and he's to watch.
	Three else of Cyprus – noble swelling spirits,
	That hold their honours in a wary distance,
	The very elements of this warlike isle – **50**
	Have I tonight flustered with flowing cups.
	And they watch too. Now, 'mongst this flock of drunkards
	Am I to put our Cassio in some action
	That may offend the isle. – But here they come.

Re-enter CASSIO, *with* MONTANO *and other* GENTLEMEN,
bringing wine.

	If consequence do but approve my dream, **55**
	My boat sails freely, both with wind and stream.

Iago sings some drinking songs as Cassio becomes more drunk.

57 rouse: large drink

60 cannikin: beer mug

63 span: short period

THINK ABOUT for GCSE

Performance and staging

- If you were the director, how would you stage this scene? What sort of mood would you want to create? Think about props, furniture, extra performers and what instructions you would give to the actors.

- Apart from line 57, what are the earliest indications that Cassio is already becoming drunk? Think also about particular words or phrases that Cassio is given to utter that a drunk might have problems with. How might his growing drunkenness show in performance?

Context

- How might Shakespeare's audiences have reacted to lines 67 to 74?

68 potent in potting: heavy drinkers
69 swag-bellied Hollander: Dutchman with a beer-belly

71 exquisite: excellent / skilled
72 with facility: easily
73 sweats not: doesn't have to make an effort
Almain: German

76 do you justice: match your toast

81 lown: rogue
82 wight: person

CASSIO	'Fore God, they have given me a rouse already.
MONTANO	Good faith, a little one – not past a pint, as I am a soldier.
IAGO	Some wine, ho!

    (*He sings, while pouring drinks*)
And let me the cannikin clink, clink,   60
And let me the cannikin clink –
A soldier's a man,
Man's life's but a span –
Why, then let a soldier drink!
Some wine, boys!   65

They drink.

CASSIO	'Fore God, an excellent song!
IAGO	I learned it in England, where indeed they are most potent in potting. Your Dane, your German, and your swag-bellied Hollander – drink, ho! – are nothing to your English. 70
CASSIO	Is your Englishman so exquisite in his drinking?
IAGO	Why – he drinks you with facility your Dane dead drunk – he sweats not to overthrow your Almain. He gives your Hollander a vomit ere the next pottle can be filled!
CASSIO	To the health of our general! 75
MONTANO	I am for it, lieutenant, and I'll do you justice.

They drink.

IAGO	O sweet England! –

    (*Singing again*)
King Stephen was a worthy peer –
His breeches cost him but a crown:
He held them sixpence all too dear –   80
With that he called the tailor lown.

He was a wight of high renown,
And thou art but of low degree:
'Tis pride that pulls the country down –
Then take thine old cloak about thee.   85
Some wine, ho!

Cassio leaves to take charge of the watch and Iago tells Montano that Cassio is often drunk.

94 **quality**: rank

THINK ABOUT *for* **GCSE**

Characterisation

- It is often said that people speak the truth when they are drunk. If that is so, what do lines 89 to 97 reveal about Cassio?

Themes and issues

- **Truth and deception**: How much of what Iago says about Cassio in lines 107 to 117 do you think is true and how much is lies?

106 **platform**: gun ramparts
     set the watch: mount the guard

110 **just equinox**: exact equivalent and opposite

113 **odd ... infirmity**: chance moment when he is drunk

114 **shake**: endanger

115 **'Tis ... prologue to**: It always comes before

116 **watch ... set**: i.e. stay awake for twenty-four hours

Cassio	'Fore God, this is a more exquisite song than the other!
Iago	Will you hear't again?
Cassio	No – for I hold him to be unworthy of his place that does those things. Well, God's above all – and there be souls must be saved, and there be souls must not be saved.
Iago	It's true, good lieutenant.
Cassio	For mine own part – no offence to the general, nor any man of quality – *I* hope to be saved.
Iago	And so do I too, lieutenant.
Cassio	Ay, but by your leave, not before me. The lieutenant is to be saved before the ancient. Let's have no more of this. Let's to our affairs. – God forgive us our sins! – Gentlemen, let's look to our business. Do not think, gentlemen, I am drunk. This is my ancient – this is my right hand – and this is my left hand. I am not drunk now. I can stand well enough, and I speak well enough.
Gentlemen	Excellent well!
Cassio	Why, very well then. You must not think then that I am drunk.

Exit.

Montano	To the platform, masters. Come, let's set the watch.
Iago	You see this fellow that is gone before: He's a soldier fit to stand by Caesar And give direction – and do but see his vice. 'Tis to his virtue a just equinox, The one as long as th' other. 'Tis pity of him. I fear the trust Othello puts him in, On some odd time of his infirmity, Will _hake this island.
Montano	But is he often thus?
Iago	'Tis evermore his prologue to his sleep: He'll watch the horologe a double set If drink rock not his cradle.

Line numbers: 90, 95, 100, 105, 110, 115

Iago sends Roderigo after Cassio. Suddenly Cassio re-enters, angrily pursuing Roderigo. When Montano tries to hold him back, Cassio turns on him.

125 **hazard**: risk
second: position of lieutenant
126 **ingraft infirmity**: deeply rooted weakness

THINK ABOUT for GCSE

Characterisation
- What do we learn about Cassio here? What might Roderigo have said or done to make Cassio angry? Look at lines 134 to 135, for example. What causes Cassio to forget Roderigo and start fighting with Montano?

131 **Zounds**: By God's wounds (a powerful oath)

Performance and staging
- What are the difficulties of staging this part of the scene (lines 117 to 139)? Think, for example, about (a) Iago's asides to Roderigo; (b) keeping up the pace while allowing the audience to see and hear what is happening; and (c) staging the struggles and the fight.

136 **prate**: complain / talk

139 **mazzard**: head

MONTANO	It were well
	The general were put in mind of it.
	Perhaps he sees it not, or his good nature
	Prizes the virtue that appears in Cassio 120
	And looks not on his evils. Is not this true?

Enter RODERIGO.

| IAGO | (*Aside to* RODERIGO) How now, Roderigo? |
| | I pray you – after the lieutenant – go! |

Exit RODERIGO.

MONTANO	– And 'tis great pity that the noble Moor
	Should hazard such a place as his own second 125
	With one of an ingraft infirmity.
	It were an honest action to say so
	To the Moor.

IAGO	Not I, for this fair island!
	I do love Cassio well and would do much
	To cure him of this evil.

Sudden cries – Help! Help! – *are heard.*

| | – But hark? What noise?   130 |

Re-enter RODERIGO, *running, pursued by* CASSIO.

| CASSIO | Zounds! – you rogue! You rascal! |

| MONTANO | What's the matter, lieutenant? |

| CASSIO | A knave teach me my duty? I'll beat the knave into a |
| | wicker bottle! |

| RODERIGO | Beat me?   135 |

| CASSIO | Dost thou prate, rogue? |

He strikes RODERIGO.

| MONTANO | Nay, good lieutenant! (*Trying to restrain* CASSIO) I pray |
| | you, sir, hold your hand. |

| CASSIO | Let me go, sir – or I'll knock *you* o'er the mazzard! |

| MONTANO | Come, come, you're drunk!   140 |

Cassio and Montano fight. Iago sends Roderigo to go and raise the alarm. Othello enters and attempts to find out how the brawl started. Iago claims that he does not know.

THINK ABOUT for GCSE

Structure and form
- Which of Iago's actions here cleverly converts a small-scale brawl into something that will disturb the whole island?

Performance and staging
- Occasionally Shakespeare includes a description in the dialogue that acts as a stage direction. According to the end of Othello's main speech, how should Iago be behaving here?

Language
- Why might Iago have deliberately chosen to describe Cassio and Montano as 'in terms like bride and groom / Divesting them for bed' (lines 165 to 166)? What effect might the image have on Othello?

142 **cry a mutiny**: shout out that there's a riot

146 **Diablo**: The devil

148 **shamed**: dishonoured / humiliated

150 **He dies**: I'll kill him

157 **heaven … Ottomites**: God prevented the Turks from doing
159 **carve … rage**: strike with his sword, prompted by anger
160 **Holds … light**: does not put much value on his life
161 **dreadful**: frightening
162 **propriety**: usual peaceful state
164 **charge**: order
165 **even now**: only a moment ago
166 **quarter**: 1 conduct; 2 friendship
      terms: relationship
167 **Divesting**: getting undressed
168 **unwitted men**: turned men mad

CASSIO	Drunk?

He draws his sword to attack MONTANO. *They fight.*

IAGO	(*Aside to* RODERIGO) Away, I say! Go out and cry a mutiny!

Exit RODERIGO.

Nay, good lieutenant! – God's will, gentlemen!
Help, ho! Lieutenant – sir! – Montano!
Help, masters! Here's a goodly watch indeed!   145

The alarm bell of the fortress begins to ring.

Who's that which rings the bell? Diablo, ho! –
The town will rise. God's will, lieutenant –
You will be shamed for ever!

Enter OTHELLO, *and attendants with weapons.*

OTHELLO	What is the matter here?
MONTANO	Zounds, I bleed still! I am hurt to the death. (*Attacking* CASSIO *again*) He dies! 150
OTHELLO	Hold! – for your lives!
IAGO	Hold, ho! Lieutenant – sir – Montano! – Gentlemen! Have you forgot all sense of place and duty? Hold! The general speaks to you. Hold, for shame!
OTHELLO	Why, how now, ho? From whence ariseth this? 155 Are we turned Turks, and to ourselves do that Which heaven hath forbid the Ottomites? For Christian shame put by this barbarous brawl! He that stirs next to carve for his own rage Holds his soul light: he dies upon his motion! 160 Silence that dreadful bell. It frights the isle From her propriety. What is the matter, masters? Honest Iago, that looks dead with grieving – Speak. Who began this? On thy love, I charge thee.
IAGO	I do not know. Friends all but now, even now – 165 In quarter and in terms like bride and groom Divesting them for bed. And then, but now – As if some planet had unwitted men –

Unable to get a clear explanation from Cassio or Montano, Othello turns to Iago.

169 **tilting**: thrusting

171 **peevish odds**: senseless quarrel
172 **would**: I wish

174 **are thus forgot**: have forgotten yourself like this

176 **were ... civil**: used to be well-mannered
177 **gravity**: seriousness
      stillness: level-headedness
179 **censure**: judgement
181 **spend ... opinion**: lose the high reputation you have earned

183 **hurt to danger**: seriously wounded

185 **something ... offends**: is somewhat painful to
186 **aught**: anything

188 **self-charity**: self-defence

THINK ABOUT for GCSE

Characterisation
• What does Othello do or say here which suggests that he becomes infuriated when he doesn't get a straight answer to a question? How might Iago exploit this weakness later?

Language
• How does the language in lines 193 to 195 (from 'If I stir') help the actor to deliver the lines in a firm and commanding manner? Think about the lengths of words and the rhythm of the lines.

191 **blood**: anger
192 **collied**: darkened / clouded
193 **Assays**: attempts

195 **sink ... rebuke**: will suffer my punishment
196 **foul rout**: shameful brawl
197 **approved in**: found guilty of
199 **lose me**: i.e. lose my friendship and support

202 **on ... safety**: in the guard house and on watch duty

	Swords out, and tilting one at other's breasts	
	In opposition bloody. I cannot speak	170
	Any beginning to this peevish odds –	
	And would in action glorious I had lost	
	These legs that brought me to a part of it!	

OTHELLO   How comes it, Michael, you are thus forgot?

CASSIO   I pray you pardon me. I cannot speak.   175

OTHELLO   Worthy Montano – you were wont be civil.
The gravity and stillness of your youth
The world hath noted, and your name is great
In mouths of wisest censure. What's the matter
That you unlace your reputation thus   180
And spend your rich opinion for the name
Of a night-brawler? Give me answer to it.

MONTANO   Worthy Othello, I am hurt to danger.
Your officer, Iago, can inform you –
While I spare speech, which something now offends
   me –   185
Of all that I do know. Nor know I aught
By me that's said or done amiss this night,
Unless self-charity be sometimes a vice,
And to defend ourselves it be a sin
When violence assails us.

OTHELLO   Now, by heaven,   190
My blood begins my safer guides to rule,
And passion, having my best judgement collied,
Assays to lead the way. Zounds! – If I stir
Or do but lift this arm, the best of you
Shall sink in my rebuke. Give me to know   195
How this foul rout began, who set it on –
And he that is approved in this offence,
Though he had twinned with me, both at a birth,
Shall lose me. What! – In a town of war
Yet wild, the people's hearts brimful of fear,   200
To manage private and domestic quarrel? –
In night, and on the court and guard of safety?
'Tis monstrous. Iago, who began it?

While seeming to be on Cassio's side, Iago manages to blame him for starting the fight. Othello dismisses Cassio as his lieutenant.

204 **partially affined**: influenced by friendship
leagued in office: i.e. siding with Cassio because of your job

206 **Touch ... near**: i.e. Don't ask me to swear on my oath as a soldier

214 **this gentleman**: i.e. Montano
215 **entreats his pause**: begs him to stop

217 **clamour**: shouting

219 **the rather**: anyway
220 **For that**: because
221 **high in oath**: swearing violently

227 **forget**: forget themselves

231 **strange indignity**: unknown insult
232 **patience ... pass**: could not be tolerated

233 **mince**: play down

THINK ABOUT for GCSE

Themes and issues

- **Reputation and honour:**
  What does Montano's speech to Iago (lines 204 to 206) reveal about a soldier's sense of honour?

- **Truth and deception:**
  Where does Iago tell a direct lie here? What is the purpose of the lie? Why can he be confident that he will not be found out?

Characterisation

- How does Iago manage to put the blame on Cassio while giving Cassio the impression that he is defending him, and showing Montano that he is giving a fair and unbiased account?

MONTANO	If partially affined, or leagued in office,
	Thou dost deliver more or less than truth,	205
	Thou art no soldier.

IAGO   Touch me not so near.
I had rather have this tongue cut from my mouth
Than it should do offence to Michael Cassio.
Yet, I persuade myself, to speak the truth
Shall nothing wrong him. This it is, general.   210
Montano and myself being in speech,
There comes a fellow crying out for help,
And Cassio following him with determined sword
To execute upon him. Sir, this gentleman
Steps in to Cassio and entreats his pause.   215
Myself the crying fellow did pursue,
Lest by his clamour – as it so fell out –
The town might fall in fright. He, swift of foot,
Outran my purpose – and I returned the rather
For that I heard the clink and fall of swords,   220
And Cassio high in oath – which till tonight
I ne'er might say before. When I came back –
For this was brief – I found them close together
At blow and thrust, even as again they were
When you yourself did part them.   225
More of this matter can I not report –
But men are men: the best sometimes forget.
Though Cassio did some little wrong to him,
As men in rage strike those that wish them best,
Yet surely Cassio I believe received   230
From him that fled some strange indignity,
Which patience could not pass.

OTHELLO   I know, Iago,
Thy honesty and love doth mince this matter,
Making it light to Cassio. Cassio – I love thee,
But never more be officer of mine.   235

Enter DESDEMONA, **with attendants.**

Look if my gentle love be not raised up.
(*To* CASSIO) I'll make thee an example.

DESDEMONA   What's the matter, dear?

Cassio is devastated because he believes that his reputation is ruined. Iago pretends to comfort him.

238   **sweeting**: darling

250   **bestial**: only animal-like

THINK ABOUT for GCSE

Themes and issues

• **Reputation and honour**: Why is reputation so important to a man like Cassio? How far do you agree with Iago's description of reputation in lines 254 to 257 as it is represented in the play?

Language

• How does Iago convince Cassio that he is his well-meaning and supportive friend here? Think about the effect of the change from verse to prose at line 245.

255   **imposition**: something laid upon us by others
257   **repute**: i.e. believe
258   **recover**: win back
258–9   **cast … mood**: dismissed because he is temporarily angry
259   **in policy**: i.e. as a public demonstration of Othello's discipline
261   **Sue to**: Plead with

264   **parrot**: nonsense
265   **discourse fustian**: talk boastful rubbish

OTHELLO	All's well now, sweeting: come away to bed.
	(*To* MONTANO) Sir, for your hurts, myself will be your
	surgeon.
	Lead him off. **240**

MONTANO is helped away.

Iago, look with care about the town,
And silence those whom this vile brawl distracted.
Come, Desdemona: 'tis the soldiers' life
To have their balmy slumbers waked with strife.

Exit, with DESDEMONA, *and all except* IAGO *and* CASSIO.

IAGO	What, are you hurt, lieutenant?	**245**
CASSIO	Ay, past all surgery.	
IAGO	Marry, God forbid!	
CASSIO	Reputation, reputation, reputation! O, I have lost my reputation! I have lost the immortal part of myself, and what remains is bestial. My reputation, Iago, my reputation!	**250**
IAGO	As I am an honest man, I had thought you had received some bodily wound. There is more sense in that than in reputation. Reputation is an idle and most false imposition, oft got without merit and lost without deserving. You have lost no reputation at all, unless you repute yourself such a loser. What, man! – there are ways to recover the general again. You are but now cast in his mood – a punishment more in policy than in malice – even so as one would beat his offenceless dog to affright an imperious lion. Sue to him again, and he's yours.	**255** **260**
CASSIO	I will rather sue to be despised than to deceive so good a commander with so light, so drunken, and so indiscreet an officer. Drunk! And speak parrot! And squabble! Swagger! Swear! And discourse fustian with one's own shadow! O thou invisible spirit of wine, if thou hast no name to be known by, let us call thee devil!	**265**
IAGO	What was he that you followed with your sword? What had he done to you?	

Iago advises Cassio to ask for Desdemona's help in getting back his post as lieutenant.

273 **nothing wherefore**: not the reason for it

275 **pleasance**: pleasure
276 **applause**: desire for approval

280 **wrath**: anger

282 **are too ... moraller**: criticise your behaviour too severely

287 **Hydra**: the many-headed mythological serpent
289 **by and by**: then
      presently: straight afterwards
290 **inordinate**: over the limit / excessive
      ingredience: contents
292 **familiar**: friendly

295 **well approved**: seen clear proof of

300 **denotement ... parts**: study of her qualities
301 **Importune**: Beg for
302 **free**: generous

THINK ABOUT
for **GCSE**

Language
- Earlier in the play Brabantio compared Othello to 'the devil', both because Othello is black, and he supposedly won Desdemona by use of witchcraft. Which 'devils' does Cassio suggest have possessed him here?
- How is the line 'I think you think I love you' (line 294) typical of Iago's language? Think about the sentence structure and the sentiment he is expressing.

Structure and form
- Look at lines 286 to 288. How has Cassio played into Iago's hands here? How does this help Iago set in motion the next phase of his plot?

CASSIO	I know not.	270
IAGO	Is't possible?	
CASSIO	I remember a mass of things, but nothing distinctly: a quarrel, but nothing wherefore. O God, that men should put an enemy in their mouths to steal away their brains! – that we should with joy, pleasance, revel, and applause transform ourselves into beasts!	275
IAGO	Why, but you are now well enough. How came you thus recovered?	
CASSIO	It hath pleased the devil drunkenness to give place to the devil wrath. One unperfectness shows me another, to make me frankly despise myself.	280
IAGO	Come, you are too severe a moraller. As the time, the place, and the condition of this country stands, I could heartily wish this had not befallen. But since it is as it is, mend it for your own good.	285
CASSIO	I will ask him for my place again: he shall tell me I am a drunkard. Had I as many mouths as Hydra, such an answer would stop them all. To be now a sensible man, by and by a fool, and presently a beast! O strange! Every inordinate cup is unblessed, and the ingredience is a devil.	290
IAGO	Come, come, good wine is a good familiar creature if it be well used. Exclaim no more against it. And, good lieutenant, I think you think I love you.	
CASSIO	I have well approved it, sir. I drunk!	295
IAGO	You or any man living may be drunk at a time, man. I'll tell you what you shall do. Our general's wife is now the general. I may say so in this respect, for that he hath devoted and given up himself to the contemplation, mark, and denotement of her parts and graces. Confess yourself freely to her. Importune her help to put you in your place again. She is of so free, so kind, so apt, so blessed a disposition that she holds it a vice in her goodness not to do more than she is requested. This broken joint between	300

Iago plans to make Othello believe that Desdemona is in love with Cassio. The more she pleads with Othello to take Cassio back, the more suspicious Othello will become.

THINK ABOUT for GCSE

Themes and issues
- What does line 308 add to the theme of **truth and deception**?

Characterisation
- What effect does Iago hope to produce in Cassio in lines 313 to 314? Compare this line with Act 2 Scene 1, lines 271 to 272: 'I must fetch his necessaries ashore'. How do these two statements show how rapidly Iago's fortunes have changed?
- How does his soliloquy (lines 316 to 342) show Iago's delight in using other people's good qualities as weapons to destroy them?

Performance and staging
- Look at Iago's questions in lines 316 to 319 and 328 to 330. What do they suggest about the way this soliloquy might be delivered on stage?

305 **entreat**: plead with
splinter: repair (with splints)
306 **lay**: bet / wager
crack: i.e. like a broken bone

309 **protest**: assure you
310 **think it freely**: believe it wholeheartedly
betimes: early
311 **beseech**: beg
undertake: take up my cause
312 **check**: reject

317 **free**: generous
318 **Probal**: probable / reasonable
320 **inclining**: good-natured / obliging
subdue: win over
321 **suit**: case / business
fruitful: generous
322 **the free elements**: nature in the wild
323 **renounce his baptism**: give up being a Christian
324 **seals … sin**: symbols of the religion that should save him from damnation
325 **enfettered**: chained
326 **list**: wants
327 **her appetite**: i.e. his sexual desire for her
328 **weak function**: i.e. his inability to resist her
329 **parallel**: i.e. in line with Iago's plot
331 **put on**: persuade / incite
332 **suggest**: tempt
334 **Plies**: begs / pleads with
336 **pestilence**: poison
337 **repeals him**: tries to get Cassio his job back
339 **undo … Moor**: i.e. the more he will stop believing her

	you and her husband entreat her to splinter – and, my 305 fortunes against any lay worth naming, this crack of your love shall grow stronger than it was before.
CASSIO	You advise me well.
IAGO	I protest, in the sincerity of love and honest kindness.
CASSIO	I think it freely – and betimes in the morning I will 310 beseech the virtuous Desdemona to undertake for me. I am desperate of my fortunes if they check me here.
IAGO	You are in the right. Good night, lieutenant: I must to the watch.
CASSIO	Good night, honest Iago. 315

Exit.

IAGO	And what's he then that says I play the villain, When this advice is free I give, and honest, Probal to thinking, and indeed the course To win the Moor again? For 'tis most easy Th' inclining Desdemona to subdue 320 In any honest suit. She's framed as fruitful As the free elements. And then for her To win the Moor – were't to renounce his baptism, All seals and symbols of redeemèd sin – His soul is so enfettered to her love 325 That she may make, unmake, do what she list, Even as her appetite shall play the god With his weak function. How am I then a villain To counsel Cassio to this parallel course, Directly to his good? Divinity of hell! 330 When devils will the blackest sins put on, They do suggest at first with heavenly shows – As I do now. For whiles this honest fool Plies Desdemona to repair his fortunes, And she for him pleads strongly to the Moor, 335 I'll pour this pestilence into his ear: That she repeals him for her body's lust. And by how much she strives to do him good, She shall undo her credit with the Moor.

Iago convinces the angry Roderigo that all is going to plan. He then plots his next moves.

THINK ABOUT for GCSE

Structure and form

- Approximately how much time has passed since the arrival in Cyprus at the beginning of Act 2 Scene 1? Look at Act 2 Scene 2, lines 9 to 10; and Iago's observation here 'By the mass, 'tis morning!' (line 357). What is the dramatic effect of these lines?

Characterisation

- In his first soliloquy Iago told us that his plan was 'engendered' (Act 1 Scene 3, line 394); by the second it was still 'confused' (Act 2 Scene 1, line 301). How clear to him are the details of his plan by the end of Act 2? What are his tactics in the short term? Look particularly at lines 333 to 342 and 361 to 366.

340 **pitch**: black, sticky tar

344 **cry**: pack
345 **cudgelled**: beaten
346 **issue**: result

348 **wit**: sense

352 **dilatory**: slowly passing

354 **cashiered**: dismissed as a soldier
355 **fair against**: quickly in

359 **billeted**: lodged

364 **awhile**: meanwhile
365 **jump**: exactly on time
366 **Soliciting**: pleading with
367 **Dull not device**: Don't slow down the plot
   coldness: lack of energy

So will I turn her virtue into pitch –   **340**
And out of her own goodness make the net
That shall enmesh them all.

Enter RODERIGO.

                                        – How now, Roderigo?

RODERIGO   I do follow here in the chase, not like a hound that
            hunts, but one that fills up the cry. My money is almost
            spent; I have been tonight exceedingly well cudgelled;   **345**
            and I think the issue will be, I shall have so much
            experience for my pains – and so, with no money at all,
            and a little more wit, return again to Venice.

IAGO   How poor are they that have not patience!
            What wound did ever heal but by degrees?   **350**
            Thou know'st we work by wit and not by witchcraft,
            And wit depends on dilatory time.
            Does't not go well? Cassio hath beaten thee,
            And thou by that small hurt hast cashiered Cassio.
            Though other things grow fair against the sun,   **355**
            Yet fruits that blossom first will first be ripe.
            Content thyself awhile. By the mass, 'tis morning!
            Pleasure and action make the hours seem short.
            Retire thee – go where thou art billeted.
            Away, I say! Thou shalt know more hereafter.   **360**
            Nay, get thee gone!

                                        Exit RODERIGO.

                        Two things are to be done:
            My wife must move for Cassio to her mistress –
            I'll set her on.
            Myself awhile to draw the Moor apart –
            And bring him jump when he may Cassio find   **365**
            Soliciting his wife. Ay, that's the way!
            Dull not device by coldness and delay.

                                                    Exit.

In this scene ...

- The Clown sends away some musicians hired by Cassio to play for Othello.
- Iago fetches Emilia for Cassio. She promises that she will arrange a meeting for him with Desdemona.

Cassio has hired some musicians to play for Othello, but the Clown sends them away.

1 **content your pains**: reward your efforts

3 **Naples**: The city was supposedly a major source of venereal disease.
4 **speak i' the nose**: 1 have a nasal voice; 2 suffer from a sexual disease

7 **marry are they**: they certainly are
8 **thereby ... tale**: there's a story about that (wordplay on 'tail', which can mean penis)

10 **wind instrument**: 1 woodwind instrument; 2 the anus
12 **for love's sake**: as an act of friendship

15 **to't**: i.e. play

THINK ABOUT for GCSE

Language
- What effect does the wordplay have here? Look at lines 4, 8 to 10, and 21 to 22. What is your opinion of it?

Structure and form
- In almost every production of *Othello* this dialogue with the Clown (lines 1 to 29) is cut. What are the arguments for and against cutting it? Think about the possible functions it serves and the difficulties it presents for a modern audience.

102

Cyprus: outside the private rooms of the fortress.

Enter CASSIO, *with* MUSICIANS.

CASSIO	Masters, play here. I will content your pains.
	Something that's brief – and bid 'Good morrow, general.'

The MUSICIANS *play.*

Enter CLOWN (*one of Othello's servants*).

CLOWN	Why, masters, have your instruments been in Naples that they speak i' the nose thus?	
MUSICIAN 1	How, sir, how?	5
CLOWN	Are these, I pray you, wind instruments?	
MUSICIAN 1	Ay, marry are they, sir.	
CLOWN	O, thereby hangs a tale.	
MUSICIAN 1	Whereby hangs a tale, sir?	
CLOWN	Marry, sir, by many a wind instrument that I know. But masters, here's money for you – and the general so likes your music that he desires you, for love's sake, to make no more noise with it.	10
MUSICIAN 1	Well sir, we will not.	
CLOWN	If you have any music that may *not* be heard, to't again. But, as they say, to *hear* music the general does not greatly care.	15
MUSICIAN 1	We have none such, sir.	
CLOWN	Then put up your pipes in your bag, for I'll away. Go – vanish into air, away!	20

The MUSICIANS *pack up and go.*

CASSIO	Dost thou hear, mine honest friend?
CLOWN	No. I hear not your honest friend. I hear *you*.

Cassio has asked to see Iago's wife, Emilia, hoping that she will be able to arrange a meeting for him with Desdemona. Emilia tells him that Desdemona has already pleaded with Othello on his behalf.

23 **keep ... quillets**: enough of your word-play
25 **entreats**: begs

27–8 **seem ... her**: arrange for her to be told

29 **In happy time**: You've come at a good moment

34 **Procure ... access**: i.e. arrange for me to see her
35 **presently**: at once

THINK ABOUT *for* GCSE

Structure and form

- Look at the end of Cassio's conversation with Iago in Act 2 Scene 3 (line 315) and lines 30 to 31 here. How much time has passed since Cassio's last appearance? What is the effect of these specific references to time?

Context

- In Act 1 Scene 1, line 18, Iago pointed out that Cassio was 'a Florentine'. What point is Cassio himself making at line 40?

---

40 **A Florentine**: i.e. even one of my own countrymen

42 **your displeasure**: the fact that you are out of favour
44 **stoutly**: wholeheartedly
45 **he you hurt**: i.e. Montano
46 **great affinity**: related to important people
   in wholesome wisdom: acting sensibly
47 **might not but**: cannot do anything except

CASSIO	Prithee keep up thy quillets. There's a poor piece of gold for thee. If the gentlewoman that attends the general's wife be stirring, tell her there's one Cassio entreats 25 her a little favour of speech. Wilt thou do this?
CLOWN	She is stirring, sir. If she will stir hither, I shall seem to notify unto her.
CASSIO	Do, good my friend.

Exit CLOWN.

Enter IAGO.

CASSIO	In happy time, Iago.
IAGO	You have not been abed then? 30
CASSIO	Why no: the day had broke before we parted. I have made bold, Iago, to send in to your wife. My suit to her is that she will to virtuous Desdemona Procure me some access.
IAGO	I'll send her to you presently – 35 And I'll devise a mean to draw the Moor Out of the way, that your converse and business May be more free.
CASSIO	I humbly thank you for't.

Exit IAGO.

– I never knew
A Florentine more kind and honest. 40

Enter EMILIA.

EMILIA	Good morrow, good lieutenant. I am sorry For your displeasure; but all will sure be well. The general and his wife are talking of it, And she speaks for you stoutly. The Moor replies That he you hurt is of great fame in Cyprus 45 And great affinity, and that in wholesome wisdom He might not but refuse you. But he protests he loves you,

Cassio asks to see Desdemona alone. Emilia invites him in to see Desdemona.

49 **take ... front**: seize the first safe opportunity

55 **bosom**: private feelings

much ... you: greatly in your debt

THINK ABOUT for GCSE

Characterisation
- What are your impressions so far of Iago's wife, Emilia? Look at this scene as well as her earlier appearance in Act 2 Scene 1, from line 82 onwards.

Performance and staging
- If you were the director, how would you want Cassio to perform this scene? For example, should he be nervous or confident? How should he behave towards the Clown and Emilia?

And needs no other suitor but his likings
To take the safest occasion by the front
To bring you in again.

CASSIO   Yet I beseech you,   50
If you think fit, or that it may be done,
Give me advantage of some brief discourse
With Desdemona alone.

EMILIA   Pray you, come in.
I will bestow you where you shall have time
To speak your bosom freely.

CASSIO   I am much bound to you.   55

                                                        Exeunt.

In this scene ...

• Othello gives Iago some letters to send to the Senate in Venice. He leaves to inspect the fortress's defences.

1 **pilot**: captain of the ship returning to Venice
2 **do my duties**: pay my respects
3 **works**: fortifications
4 **Repair**: Return

THINK ABOUT for GCSE

Structure and form
• What are the functions of this short scene? For example, think about the scenes which precede and follow it.

Performance and staging
• If you were directing the play on the stage of Shakespeare's Globe, where would you have this scene take place and why?

The gates of the fortress.

Enter OTHELLO, IAGO *and* GENTLEMEN.

OTHELLO	These letters give, Iago, to the pilot –
	And by him do my duties to the Senate.
	That done, I will be walking on the works.
	Repair there to me.
IAGO	Well, my good lord, I'll do't.

Exit IAGO.

OTHELLO	This fortification, gentlemen, shall we see't?	5
GENTLEMEN	We'll wait upon your lordship.	

Exeunt.

In this scene ...

- Desdemona begs Othello to take Cassio back as his lieutenant.
- Iago arouses Othello's suspicions about Desdemona and Cassio's relationship. When Desdemona loses her handkerchief, Emilia gives it to Iago, who plans to drop it in Cassio's lodgings.
- Iago tells Othello that Cassio called out Desdemona's name in his sleep and also had her handkerchief.
- Iago swears to help Othello in his jealous revenge and promises to kill Cassio. Othello makes Iago his lieutenant.

Desdemona agrees to do all she can to help Cassio get back his position as lieutenant.

4 the cause were his: it were his problem

12 strangeness: coldness / reserve
13 politic: i.e. Othello has to be seen to be keeping his distance from Cassio

15 nice: thin
16 breed ... circumstances: continue because of day-to-day happenings
17 supplied: filled
19 doubt: fear
20 warrant: guarantee
22 article: detail
23 watch him tame: i.e. keep pestering him until he does what I want
24 board: dining table
shrift: place where a priest hears confession
27 solicitor: person who argues on your behalf (i.e. Desdemona)
28 give ... away: give up your case

THINK ABOUT for GCSE

Themes and issues
- **Truth and deception**: Which lines at the beginning of this scene show how people completely fail to realise what Iago is really like?

Structure and form
- In what ways are Cassio and Desdemona doing exactly what Iago wants them to do here?

Inside the fortress.

Enter DESDEMONA, CASSIO, *and* EMILIA.

DESDEMONA	Be thou assured, good Cassio, I will do All my abilities in thy behalf.
EMILIA	Good madam, do. I know it grieves my husband As if the cause were his.
DESDEMONA	O, that's an honest fellow. Do not doubt, Cassio, 5 But I will have my lord and you again As friendly as you were.
CASSIO	Bounteous madam, Whatever shall become of Michael Cassio, He's never anything but your true servant.
DESDEMONA	I know't; I thank you. You do love my lord, 10 You have known him long, and be you well assured He shall in strangeness stand no farther off Than in a politic distance.
CASSIO	Ay, but, lady, That policy may either last so long, Or feed upon such nice and waterish diet, 15 Or breed itself so out of circumstances, That I being absent, and my place supplied, My general will forget my love and service.
DESDEMONA	Do not doubt that. Before Emilia here I give thee warrant of thy place. Assure thee, 20 If I do vow a friendship, I'll perform it To the last article. My lord shall never rest; I'll watch him tame and talk him out of patience. His bed shall seem a school, his board a shrift; I'll intermingle everything he does 25 With Cassio's suit. Therefore be merry, Cassio, For thy solicitor shall rather die Than give thy cause away.

As he enters with Othello, Iago comments on Cassio's sudden departure. Desdemona asks Othello to call Cassio back, but he refuses.

34 your discretion: whatever you think best

THINK ABOUT
for GCSE

Performance and staging

- What does Iago say in lines 35 to 40 that shows he is trying to make Othello suspicious of Cassio? How should Iago say these lines?

- If you were the director, how would you have Othello react to Iago's comments in lines 35 to 40 and to Desdemona's appeal on Cassio's behalf in lines 41 to 54?

43 languishes: suffers / wastes away

46 grace: favour in your eyes
47 His ... take: accept his repentance immediately
49 errs: makes mistakes
  in cunning: deliberately

Enter, at a distance, OTHELLO *and* IAGO.

EMILIA	Madam, here comes my lord.
CASSIO	Madam, I'll take my leave. **30**
DESDEMONA	Why, stay and hear me speak.
CASSIO	Madam, not now. I am very ill at ease – Unfit for mine own purposes.
DESDEMONA	Well, do your discretion.

Exit CASSIO.

IAGO	Ha! I like not that.
OTHELLO	What dost thou say? **35**
IAGO	Nothing, my lord; or if – I know not what.
OTHELLO	Was not that Cassio parted from my wife?
IAGO	Cassio, my lord? No, sure, I cannot think it, That he would steal away so guilty-like, Seeing you coming.
OTHELLO	I do believe 'twas he. **40**
DESDEMONA	How now, my lord? I have been talking with a suitor here, A man that languishes in your displeasure.
OTHELLO	Who is't you mean?
DESDEMONA	Why, your lieutenant, Cassio. Good my lord, **45** If I have any grace or power to move you, His present reconciliation take. For if he be not one that truly loves you, That errs in ignorance, and not in cunning, I have no judgement in an honest face. **50** I prithee call him back.
OTHELLO	Went he hence now?
DESDEMONA	Yes, faith – so humbled That he hath left part of his grief with me To suffer with him. Good love, call him back.
OTHELLO	Not now, sweet Desdemona – some other time. **55**

Desdemona continues in her efforts to persuade Othello to have a meeting with Cassio. Othello agrees to her request and in return asks to be left alone.

THINK ABOUT
for GCSE

Structure and form

- How does the structure of lines 56 to 59 help the actors get the meaning across? How should these lines be performed?

Relationships

- What do lines 70 to 74 tell us about the friendship between Othello and Cassio? How might this knowledge affect Iago, who is listening? Think about how it would make him feel and how he might use this knowledge.

---

63 he's penitent: he truly regrets what he has done

64 trespass: offence / wrongdoing

65–6 the wars ... best: in wartime even the highest-ranking people have to be made an example of

66 not almost: hardly

67 T' incur ... check: to receive a private telling off

70 mammering: stammering hesitantly

73 part: side

74 bring him in: i.e. give him back his rank of lieutenant

76 boon: favour

79–80 sue ... person: beg you to do something for your own good

80 suit: request

82–3 full ... granted: important, hard to decide upon and difficult to grant

84 Whereon: In return for which
beseech: beg

DESDEMONA	But shall't be shortly?
OTHELLO	The sooner, sweet, for you.
DESDEMONA	Shall't be tonight at supper?
OTHELLO	No, not tonight.
DESDEMONA	Tomorrow dinner then?
OTHELLO	I shall not dine at home. I meet the captains at the citadel.

DESDEMONA   Why then, tomorrow night, or Tuesday morn –   **60**
On Tuesday noon or night, or Wednesday morn.
I prithee name the time, but let it not
Exceed three days. In faith, he's penitent.
And yet his trespass, in our common reason
(Save that they say the wars must make example   **65**
Out of their best), is not almost a fault
T' incur a private check. When shall he come?
Tell me, Othello. I wonder in my soul
What you would ask me that I should deny,
Or stand so mammering on. What! Michael Cassio,   **70**
That came a-wooing with you, and so many a time,
When I have spoke of you dispraisingly,
Hath ta'en your part – to have so much to do
To bring him in? By'r Lady, I could do much –

OTHELLO   Prithee no more. Let him come when he will.   **75**
I will deny thee nothing.

DESDEMONA   Why, this is not a boon.
'Tis as I should entreat you wear your gloves,
Or feed on nourishing dishes, or keep you warm,
Or sue to you to do a peculiar profit
To your own person. Nay – when I have a suit   **80**
Wherein I mean to touch your love indeed,
It shall be full of poise and difficult weight,
And fearful to be granted.

OTHELLO   I will deny thee nothing!
Whereon I do beseech thee, grant me this,
To leave me but a little to myself.   **85**

DESDEMONA   Shall I deny you? No. Farewell, my lord.

When Desdemona leaves, Iago asks how much Cassio knew of Othello's courtship of Desdemona.

87   **straight**: straight away

88   **Be as … you**: i.e. Do whatever you feel like

90   **Perdition … soul**: May my soul be damned

91   **But I do**: if I do not
     when … not: if ever I were not to love you

92   **Chaos … again**: it would be the end of the world

102   **Discern'st thou aught**: Do you see anything

104   **for aught I know**: as far as I'm aware

THINK ABOUT for GCSE

Relationships
- What do lines 90 to 92 tell us about the nature of Othello's love for Desdemona?

Language
- Look at Iago's clever use of language. What reaction does he hope to create by (a) saying 'Indeed?' (line 101); (b) pretending to avoid straight answers by repeating Othello's questions (lines 103 and 105); and (c) giving non-committal answers (line 104)?

OTHELLO	Farewell, my Desdemona. I'll come to thee straight.
DESDEMONA	Emilia, come. (*To* OTHELLO) Be as your fancies teach you: Whate'er you be, I am obedient.

Exit, with EMILIA.

OTHELLO	Excellent wretch! Perdition catch my soul But I do love thee! And when I love thee not, Chaos is come again.	90
IAGO	My noble lord –	
OTHELLO	What dost thou say, Iago?	
IAGO	Did Michael Cassio, when you wooed my lady, Know of your love?	95
OTHELLO	He did, from first to last. Why dost thou ask?	
IAGO	But for a satisfaction of my thought – No further harm.	
OTHELLO	Why of thy thought, Iago?	
IAGO	I did not think he had been acquainted with her.	
OTHELLO	Oh, yes – and went between us very oft.	100
IAGO	Indeed?	
OTHELLO	Indeed? Ay, indeed! Discern'st thou aught in that? Is he not honest?	
IAGO	Honest, my lord?	
OTHELLO	Honest? Ay, honest.	
IAGO	My lord, for aught I know.	
OTHELLO	What dost thou think?	
IAGO	Think, my lord?	105
OTHELLO	Think, my lord! – By heaven, he echoes me, As if there were some monster in his thought Too hideous to be shown! Thou dost mean something. I heard thee say but now thou lik'st not that, When Cassio left my wife. What didst not like?	110

Having raised doubts about
Cassio, Iago refuses to tell
Othello what is on his mind,
but implies that his thoughts are
unpleasant.

111   **of my counsel**: trusted with my secrets

113   **contract ... together**: frown

115   **conceit**: idea / thought

120   **stops**: sudden pauses

122   **of custom**: customary / usual
      just: honest
123   **close dilations**: hesitant expressions of
      secret thoughts

THINK ABOUT for GCSE

Performance and staging

• Shakespeare often gives
  stage directions to actors
  through his characters'
  speeches. Which of
  Othello's lines suggest how
  the actor playing Iago should
  have reacted at line 101?

Language

• Look at the replies Iago gives
  about Cassio in lines 124
  to 125 and 129. What is he
  trying to achieve by phrasing
  his replies in this way?

• How does the legal imagery
  in lines 140 to 141 help
  to convey the idea that
  even the purest people
  can occasionally have bad
  thoughts?

127   **seem none**: 1 not seem to be men;
      2 not seem to be honest men

131   **speak ... thinkings**: tell me what is in
      your mind
132   **ruminate**: think things through

135   **that ... to**: the right that slaves have to
      keep their thoughts to themselves
137   **As**: for example
139   **uncleanly apprehensions**: filthy thoughts
140   **leets and law days**: sessions of local
      law courts
141   **meditations lawful**: innocent thoughts

	And when I told thee he was of my counsel	
	In my whole course of wooing, thou cried'st 'Indeed?'	
	And didst contract and purse thy brow together,	
	As if thou then hadst shut up in thy brain	
	Some horrible conceit. If thou dost love me,	115
	Show me thy thought.	

IAGO   My lord, you know I love you.

OTHELLO   I think thou dost –
And, for I know thou'rt full of love and honesty
And weigh'st thy words before thou giv'st them breath,
Therefore these stops of thine fright me the more.   120
For such things in a false disloyal knave
Are tricks of custom; but in a man that's just
They're close dilations, working from the heart,
That passion cannot rule.

IAGO   For Michael Cassio,
I dare be sworn, I think that he is honest.   125

OTHELLO   I think so too.

IAGO   Men should be what they seem –
Or those that be not, would they might seem none!

OTHELLO   Certain, men should be what they seem.

IAGO   Why then, I think Cassio's an honest man.

OTHELLO   Nay, yet there's more in this.   130
I prithee speak to me as to thy thinkings,
As thou dost ruminate, and give thy worst of thoughts
The worst of words.

IAGO   Good my lord, pardon me.
Though I am bound to every act of duty,
I am not bound to that all slaves are free to.   135
Utter my thoughts? Why, say they are vile and false –
As where's that palace whereinto foul things
Sometimes intrude not? Who has that breast so pure
But some uncleanly apprehensions
Keep leets and law days, and in sessions sit   140
With meditations lawful?

Iago continues to seem reluctant to tell Othello what he is thinking. He introduces the subject of reputation and warns Othello to beware of jealousy.

147 **jealousy**: suspicious mind
148 **Shapes**: imagines
149 **imperfectly conceits**: imagines things mistakenly or only in part
151 **scattering**: random
152 **quiet**: peace of mind

155 **Good name**: Reputation
156 **immediate jewel**: most precious personal possession

159 **filches**: steals

163 **if**: even if

167 **cuckold**: man whose wife has been unfaithful
168 **his wronger**: i.e. the wife betraying him
169 **tells**: counts

THINK ABOUT for GCSE

Language
- How does the sentence structure of lines 144 to 151 help Iago to sound reluctant and hesitant? Look at the lengths of the sentences and the clauses beginning 'Though' and 'As'.

Themes and issues
- Iago makes one of Shakespeare's most memorable statements about **reputation** in lines 155 to 161. What does he say?
- In what ways is Iago's 'Good name' speech (lines 155 to 161) both a **truth** and a **deception**? Think about the context in which he is offering advice.

OTHELLO	Thou dost conspire against thy friend, Iago,
	If thou but *think'st* him wronged, and mak'st his ear
	A stranger to thy thoughts.
IAGO	I do beseech you –
	Though I perchance am vicious in my guess **145**
	(As I confess it is my nature's plague
	To spy into abuses, and oft my jealousy
	Shapes faults that are not) – that your wisdom yet
	From one that so imperfectly conceits
	Would take no notice, nor build yourself a trouble **150**
	Out of his scattering and unsure observance.
	It were not for your quiet nor your good,
	Nor for my manhood, honesty, and wisdom,
	To let you know my thoughts.
OTHELLO	What dost thou mean?
IAGO	Good name in man and woman, dear my lord, **155**
	Is the immediate jewel of their souls.
	Who steals my purse steals trash: 'tis something, nothing –
	'Twas mine, 'tis his – and has been slave to thousands.
	But he that filches from me my good name
	Robs me of that which not enriches him **160**
	And makes *me* poor indeed.
OTHELLO	By heaven, I'll know thy thoughts!
IAGO	You cannot, if my heart were in your hand –
	Nor shall not, whilst 'tis in my custody.
OTHELLO	Ha!
IAGO	O beware, my lord, of jealousy! **165**
	It is the green-eyed monster, which doth mock
	The meat it feeds on. That cuckold lives in bliss
	Who, certain of his fate, loves not his wronger.
	But O, what damnèd minutes tells he o'er
	Who dotes, yet doubts – suspects, yet strongly loves! **170**
OTHELLO	O misery!

Othello claims that he would never let jealousy take control of him. Pretending to be reassured by this statement, Iago tells Othello to keep a close watch on Desdemona and Cassio.

173   **fineless**: limitless
174   **ever**: always

178–9   **follow ... suspicions**: i.e. have fresh suspicions with each phase of the moon
180   **once**: once and for all
       resolved: free from doubt / convinced
182   **exsufflicate ... surmises**: exaggerated and inflated assumptions
183   **Matching thy inference**: as you suggest

THINK ABOUT *for*GCSE

Language
- Without making any direct accusations Iago manages to make Othello suspect that he has been deceived. How does he do this? Look at the development of Iago's argument in lines 155 to 170, focusing particularly on lines 155, 165 and 167.
- What is the effect of the word 'yet' in line 196?

Context
- In Shakespeare's time, Venetian women had a reputation for loose sexual morals. How does Iago use this reputation, and Othello's inexperience with women, to make him feel insecure (lines 201 to 204)?

188   **doubt**: suspicion
       revolt: unfaithfulness
190   **doubt**: suspect

195   **as I am bound**: since it is my duty

198   **jealous**: over-suspicious
       secure: over-confident
199   **free**: generous
200   **self-bounty**: natural generosity
201   **country disposition**: i.e. sexual behaviour of Venetian women
203   **best conscience**: highest idea of morality

IAGO	Poor and content is rich, and rich enough –
	But riches fineless is as poor as winter
	To him that ever fears he shall be poor.
	Good God, the souls of all my tribe defend 175
	From jealousy!

OTHELLO
                    Why? Why is this?
            Think'st thou I'd make a life of jealousy? –
            To follow still the changes of the moon
            With fresh suspicions? No! To be once in doubt
            Is once to be resolved. Exchange me for a goat   180
            When I shall turn the business of my soul
            To such exsufflicate and blown surmises,
            Matching thy inference. 'Tis not to make me jealous
            To say my wife is fair, feeds well, loves company,
            Is free of speech, sings, plays, and dances well.   185
            Where virtue is, these are more virtuous.
            Nor from mine own weak merits will I draw
            The smallest fear or doubt of her revolt –
            For she had eyes, and chose me. No, Iago.
            I'll see before I doubt; when I doubt, prove;   190
            And on the proof there is no more but this:
            Away at once with love or jealousy!

IAGO
            I am glad of this – for now I shall have reason
            To show the love and duty that I bear you
            With franker spirit. Therefore, as I am bound,   195
            Receive it from me. I speak not yet of proof.
            Look to your wife: observe her well with Cassio.
            Wear your eyes thus – not jealous, nor secure.
            I would not have your free and noble nature
            Out of self-bounty be abused. Look to't.   200
            I know our country disposition well:
            In Venice they do let Heaven see the pranks
            They dare not show their husbands. Their best
                  conscience
            Is not to leave't undone, but keep't unknown.

OTHELLO   Dost thou say so?   205

IAGO   She did deceive her father, marrying you –
            And when she seemed to shake and fear your looks,
            She loved them most.

Seeing how upset Othello is, Iago claims that everything he says is out of friendship. He points out how strange it was that Desdemona did not marry someone with a similar background to herself.

208 go to: there you are

210 seel: close up
close as oak: as tightly as the grain in oak

213 bound to thee: in your debt

THINK ABOUT for GCSE

Language

• Think about the dramatic irony of 'I am bound to thee for ever' in line 213. What does Othello mean by 'bound' and what other meaning can it have?

Themes and issues

• **Truth and deception**: Knowing that Othello believes him to be 'honest', Iago can easily fool Othello into thinking that he is covering up an unpleasant truth out of loyalty to Cassio or Desdemona. How effectively does he do this in lines 221 to 226?

• **Race**: How might Iago's references to Desdemona's 'clime, complexion and degree' in line 230 make Othello feel an outsider?

217 moved: disturbed
218 am to: must
strain: stretch the meaning of
219 grosser: 1 wider; 2 to do with sex
issues: conclusions
larger: 1 broader; 2 sexually coarser

222 fall ... success: have evil consequences

225 honest: sexually virtuous / chaste

227 erring from itself: straying from its true course

229 affect: like / be attracted by
230 clime ... degree: country, colour and rank
232 will: 1 intention; 2 sexual desire
rank: 1 bad; 2 lustful
233 disproportion: abnormality / perversion
234–5 in position ... her: refer specifically to her (i.e. to Desdemona)

OTHELLO	And so she did.
IAGO	Why – go to then!
	She that so young could give out such a seeming
	To seel her father's eyes up close as oak – 210
	He thought 'twas witchcraft. – But I am much to blame.
	I humbly do beseech you of your pardon
	For too much loving you.
OTHELLO	I am bound to thee for ever.
IAGO	I see this hath a little dashed your spirits.
OTHELLO	Not a jot, not a jot.
IAGO	Trust me, I fear it has. 215
	I hope you will consider what is spoke
	Comes from my love. But I do see you're moved.
	I am to pray you not to strain my speech
	To grosser issues, nor to larger reach
	Than to suspicion. 220
OTHELLO	I will not.
IAGO	Should you do so, my lord,
	My speech should fall into such vile success
	As my thoughts aimed not at. Cassio's my worthy
	friend –
	My lord, I see you're moved.
OTHELLO	No – not much moved.
	I do not think but Desdemona's honest. 225
IAGO	Long live she so! And long live you to think so.
OTHELLO	And yet how nature, erring from itself –
IAGO	Ay, there's the point – as (to be bold with you)
	Not to affect many proposèd matches
	Of her own clime, complexion, and degree, 230
	Whereto we see in all things nature tends –
	Foh! – One may smell in such a will most rank,
	Foul disproportion, thoughts unnatural.
	But pardon me. I do not in position
	Distinctly speak of her – though I may fear 235

Iago leaves, advising Othello to be suspicious if Desdemona begs him to give Cassio his job back. Othello begins to think of reasons why Desdemona might have grown tired of him.

236 recoiling: returning

237 fall … forms: start to compare you with how Venetians look

238 happily repent: perhaps regret (marrying you)

244 would: wish
    entreat: persuade

245 scan: keep examining

THINK ABOUT for GCSE

Characterisation

• Iago often urges Othello to do something knowing that it will encourage him to take the opposite action. How effectively does Iago use this tactic at lines 218 to 223 and 244 to 245?

• Which of Othello's comments show how very quickly he has lost confidence in Desdemona's love for him? What three reasons does he give here to explain her possible unfaithfulness?

Language

• What does the falconry image in lines 259 to 262 reveal about Othello's attitude to Desdemona at this point in the play?

249 means: methods (to get his job back)

250 strain his entertainment: begs you to take him back

251 vehement importunity: forceful pleading

253 too … fears: over-suspicious

255 hold her free: believe her to be innocent

256 government: self control

259 haggard: like a wild, untrainable hawk

260 jesses: Leather straps that held the hawk's legs to the falconer's hand.

261 whistle her off: set her free

262 prey at fortune: fend for herself
    Haply for: Perhaps because

263 soft … conversation: attractive social skills

264 chamberers: 'ladies' men' / courtiers

264–5 declined … years: getting old

266 abused: deceived

Her will, recoiling to her better judgement,
May fall to match you with her country forms,
And happily repent.

OTHELLO   Farewell, farewell. –
If more thou dost perceive, let me know more.
Set on thy wife to observe. Leave me, Iago.   **240**

IAGO   (*Going*) My lord, I take my leave.

OTHELLO   Why did I marry? This honest creature doubtless
Sees and knows more, much more, than he unfolds.

IAGO   (*Returning*) My lord, I would I might entreat your honour
To scan this thing no farther. Leave it to time.   **245**
Although 'tis fit that Cassio have his place –
For sure he fills it up with great ability –
Yet, if you please to hold him off awhile,
You shall by that perceive him and his means.
Note if your lady strain his entertainment   **250**
With any strong or vehement importunity:
Much will be seen in that. In the meantime
Let me be thought too busy in my fears
(As worthy cause I have to fear I am)
And hold her free, I do beseech your honour.   **255**

OTHELLO   Fear not my government.

IAGO   I once more take my leave.

Exit.

OTHELLO   This fellow's of exceeding honesty,
And knows all qualities, with a learnèd spirit,
Of human dealings. If I do prove her haggard,
Though that her jesses were my dear heart-strings,   **260**
I'd whistle her off, and let her down the wind
To prey at fortune. Haply for I am black
And have not those soft parts of conversation
That chamberers have – or for I am declined
Into the vale of years – yet that's not much –   **265**
She's gone. – I am abused – and my relief
Must be to loathe her. O curse of marriage –
That we can call these delicate creatures ours,

Desdemona enters. She is concerned that Othello seems unwell and offers him her handkerchief, which was a gift from him. It falls to the ground and Emilia picks it up.

273 **Prerogatived … base**: i.e. public figures are in a worse position than common people (because their shame is greater)
274 **unshunnable**: unavoidable / inevitable
275 **forkèd**: horned (It was a common belief that a cuckold grew horns.)
276 **do quicken**: are born

279 **generous**: noble
280 **attend**: wait for

THINK ABOUT for GCSE

Context

- In Shakespeare's time there was a belief that a cuckold – a man whose wife was unfaithful – would grow horns (the 'forkèd plague' of line 275) that all but he could see. How effectively do lines 267 to 276 express Othello's fear of being made a cuckold? What in particular does he seem to dread about it?

Characterisation

- What does Desdemona's response to Othello's behaviour suggest about her? What is your opinion of the way she reacts?

283 **forehead**: He is also referring to the growing cuckold's horns.
284 **watching**: lack of sleep
285 **hard**: tightly

286 **napkin**: handkerchief

290 **remembrance**: gift
291 **wayward**: unpredictable
292 **Wooed**: persuaded
293 **conjured her**: made her swear
294 **reserves**: keeps
295 **work ta'en out**: embroidery copied

And not their appetites! I had rather be a toad
And live upon the vapour of a dungeon,   270
Than keep a corner in the thing I love
For others' uses. Yet 'tis the plague of great ones –
Prerogatived are they less than the base:
'Tis destiny unshunnable, like death.
Even then this forkèd plague is fated to us   275
When we do quicken. – Look where she comes.

Enter DESDEMONA *and* EMILIA.

– If she be false, O then heaven mocks itself!
I'll not believe it.

DESDEMONA	How now, my dear Othello?

Your dinner, and the generous islanders
By you invited, do attend your presence.   280

OTHELLO I am to blame.

DESDEMONA   Why do you speak so faintly?
Are you not well?

OTHELLO I have a pain upon my forehead, here.

DESDEMONA Why, that's with watching: 'twill away again.
Let me but bind it hard, within this hour   285
It will be well.

OTHELLO   Your napkin is too little.

He brushes her handkerchief aside, and she drops it.

– Let it alone. Come, I'll go in with you.

DESDEMONA I am very sorry that you are not well.

Exit, with OTHELLO.

EMILIA I am glad I have found this napkin:
This was her first remembrance from the Moor.   290
My wayward husband hath a hundred times
Wooed me to steal it – but she so loves the token
(For he conjured her she should ever keep it)
That she reserves it evermore about her
To kiss and talk to. I'll have the work ta'en out   295

Iago takes Desdemona's handkerchief from Emilia. He has asked her to get it many times before, but refuses to say why he wants it.

THINK ABOUT for GCSE

Structure and form

- *Othello* has a strange double time-scheme: some comments suggest that only a few days have passed since the play began, making the play seem fast-paced. However, other comments imply that Othello has been married to Desdemona for quite a while, making the plot more believable. How do lines 289 to 298 help to give the impression that Iago has been planning his revenge on the married Othello for quite a while?

Relationships

- What do we learn about the relationship between Emilia and Iago from Emilia's comment in line 298 and from the exchange between them in lines 299 to 318?

Performance and staging

- If you were the director, how would you stage this exchange?

---

298 I nothing ... fantasy: I know nothing except to serve his whims / strange ideas

300 chide: complain / scold

301 common: available to everyone
thing: can also mean a female sexual organ

311 to th' advantage: luckily

314 filch: steal

315 import: importance

317 lack: miss
Be ... on't: Say you know nothing about it

> And give it Iago.
> What he'll do with it, heaven knows, not I –
> I nothing, but to please his fantasy.

Enter IAGO.

IAGO	How now? What do you here alone?
EMILIA	Do not you chide. I have a thing for you.
IAGO	You have a thing for me? It is a common thing –
EMILIA	Ha!
IAGO	– To have a foolish wife.
EMILIA	O, is that all? What will you give me now For that same handkerchief?
IAGO	What handkerchief?
EMILIA	What handkerchief? Why, that the Moor first gave to Desdemona – That which so often you did bid me steal.
IAGO	Hast stolen it from her?
EMILIA	No, faith: she let it drop by negligence – And to th' advantage I, being here, took't up. Look – here it is.
IAGO	A good wench! Give it me.
EMILIA	What will you do with it, that you have been so earnest To have me filch it?
IAGO	Why – what is that to you?

He snatches the handkerchief.

EMILIA	If it be not for some purpose of import, Give't me again. Poor lady, she'll run mad When she shall lack it.
IAGO	Be not acknown on't. I have use for it. Go – leave me.

Exit EMILIA.

300

305

310

315

Iago plans to leave the handkerchief in Cassio's lodgings for him to find. Othello returns, in agony, believing Desdemona to be unfaithful.

320 **Trifles**: Irrelevant little details

322 **writ**: scripture

324 **conceits**: ideas / imaginings
325 **distaste**: taste unpleasant
326 **act**: action

328–9 **poppy ... syrups**: sleeping potions

331 **owed'st**: owned / enjoyed

333 **Avaunt**: Get out of here
    the rack: an instrument of torture

336 **sense**: awareness

THINK ABOUT for GCSE

Characterisation

* What do Iago's aside (lines 328 to 331) and Othello's opening line (line 331) suggest about Othello's appearance and behaviour as he returns?

* What is Othello's attitude to Iago at this point (lines 333 to 335)?

340 **wanting**: missing

343 **had**: would have
344 **Pioneers**: the lowest-ranking soldiers
345 **So**: if only
346 **the tranquil mind**: peace of mind
348 **makes ambition virtue**: makes it a noble thing to be ambitious
349 **trump**: trumpet
350 **fife**: soldier's flute

I will in Cassio's lodging lose this napkin
And let him find it. Trifles light as air   320
Are to the jealous confirmations strong
As proofs of holy writ. – This may do something.
The Moor already changes with my poison.
Dangerous conceits are in their natures poisons,
Which at the first are scarce found to distaste,   325
But, with a little act upon the blood,
Burn like the mines of sulphur. –

Enter OTHELLO.

                              I did say so. –
Look where he comes! Not poppy nor mandragora,
Nor all the drowsy syrups of the world,
Shall ever medicine thee to that sweet sleep   330
Which thou owed'st yesterday.

OTHELLO	Ha, ha! False to me?
IAGO	Why how now, general? No more of that.
OTHELLO	Avaunt! – be gone! Thou hast set me on the rack. I swear 'tis better to be much abused Than but to know't a little.
IAGO	How now, my lord? 335
OTHELLO	What sense had I of her stol'n hours of lust? I saw't not, thought it not – it harmed not me. I slept the next night well, fed well, was free and merry – I found not Cassio's kisses on her lips. He that is robbed, not wanting what is stol'n, 340 Let him not know't and he's not robbed at all.
IAGO	I am sorry to hear this.
OTHELLO	I had been happy if the general camp, Pioneers and all, had tasted her sweet body – So I had nothing known! O now, for ever 345 Farewell the tranquil mind! Farewell content! Farewell the plumèd troops, and the big wars That makes ambition virtue! – O, farewell! Farewell the neighing steed and the shrill trump, The spirit-stirring drum, th' ear-piercing fife, 350 The royal banner – and all quality,

Othello angrily turns on Iago, demanding proof that Desdemona is unfaithful.

THINK ABOUT for GCSE

Language
- Lines 345 to 355 contain some of Othello's grandest language. How does the language convey a sense of all the glory that Othello will never again enjoy?

Performance and staging
- In many productions, Othello physically attacks Iago at line 357. If you were the director, what effect would you want to achieve at this moment?

Characterisation
- How do Othello's words show a change in his thinking and attitude? Look at his reference to Desdemona in line 357 and the demand he makes of Iago in lines 358 to 364.

- How does Iago react when Othello comes close to accusing him (lines 371 to 381)?

352 **Pride ... circumstance**: proud displays and showy ceremony
353 **mortal engines**: deadly cannons
rude: rough
354 **Jove**: god of thunder
dread clamours: terrifying noises (i.e. thunder)
counterfeit: imitate
355 **occupation**: vocation / calling
358 **ocular**: visible
361 **wrath**: anger

363 **probation**: proof
hinge nor loop: i.e. no loop-hole or hook

373 **Take mine office**: You can have my job back
374 **vice**: weakness

377 **profit**: useful lesson
378 **sith**: since
breeds such offence: causes such harm

381 **that**: what

383 **just**: trustworthy

	Pride, pomp, and circumstance of glorious war!
	And O you mortal engines, whose rude throats
	Th' immortal Jove's dread clamours counterfeit,
	Farewell! Othello's occupation's gone!

 355

IAGO   Is't possible, my lord?

OTHELLO
Villain, be sure thou prove my love a whore!
Be sure of it! – Give me the ocular proof!
Or by the worth of mine eternal soul,
Thou hadst been better have been born a dog   360
Than answer my waked wrath!

IAGO   Is't come to this?

OTHELLO
Make me to see't – or at the least so prove it
That the probation bear no hinge nor loop
To hang a doubt on – or woe upon thy life!

IAGO   My noble lord –   365

OTHELLO
If thou dost slander her and torture me,
Never pray more – abandon all remorse.
On horror's head horrors accumulate!
Do deeds to make heaven weep, all earth amazed –
For nothing canst thou to damnation add   370
Greater than that.

IAGO   O grace! O heaven forgive me!
Are you a man? Have you a soul or sense? –
God be wi' you! Take mine office. – O wretched fool,
That lov'st to make thine honesty a vice!
O monstrous world! Take note, take note, O world! –   375
To be direct and honest is not safe.
I thank you for this profit, and from hence
I'll love no friend, sith love breeds such offence.

OTHELLO   Nay, stay. – Thou shouldst be honest.

IAGO
I should be wise; for honesty's a fool   380
And loses that it works for.

OTHELLO   By the world,
I think my wife be honest, and think she is not. –
I think that thou art just, and think thou art not.
I'll have some proof! Her name, that was as fresh

Iago points out that it would be difficult for Othello to catch Desdemona and Cassio together. However, he does agree to give Othello some evidence and claims that Cassio cried out Desdemona's name in his sleep.

385 **Dian's visage**: the face of Diana, goddess of chastity

386 **cords**: ropes

386–7 **cords … streams**: These are all methods of committing suicide.

388 **were satisfied**: had proof

393 **supervisor**: onlooker
gape on: watch open-mouthed

394 **Behold her topped**: Watch her having sex

395 **tedious difficulty**: very hard to arrange

396 **prospect**: spectacle

397 **bolster**: share a pillow

398 **More**: other

401 **prime**: sexually excited
hot: lecherous

402 **salt**: lustful
in pride: on heat

404 **imputation … circumstances**: opinion based on strong evidence

407 **living**: strong

408 **office**: job

409 **entered … cause**: become involved in this matter

410 **Pricked**: spurred on

411 **lay**: shared a bed

414 **loose of soul**: loose-tongued about their innermost feelings

419 **gripe**: seize

THINK ABOUT for GCSE

Language
- How effectively does Iago use crude language and descriptions to torment Othello here? Look at lines 393 to 403.

Context
- In Shakespeare's time, it was usual for people of the same sex to share a bed. How does Iago exploit that fact here?

	As Dian's visage, is now begrimed and black	385
	As mine own face. If there be cords or knives,	
	Poison, or fire, or suffocating streams,	
	I'll not endure it! – Would I were satisfied!	

IAGO I see, sir, you are eaten up with passion.
I do repent me that I put it to you.   390
You would be satisfied?

OTHELLO   Would! Nay, I will.

IAGO – And may – but how? How satisfied, my lord?
Would you, the supervisor, grossly gape on? –
Behold her topped?

OTHELLO   Death and damnation! O!

IAGO It were a tedious difficulty, I think,   395
To bring them to that prospect. Damn them then,
If ever mortal eyes do see them bolster
More than their own! What then? – How then?
What shall I say? – Where's satisfaction?
It is impossible you should see this,   400
Were they as prime as goats, as hot as monkeys,
As salt as wolves in pride, and fools as gross
As ignorance made drunk. But yet, I say,
If imputation and strong circumstances
Which lead directly to the door of truth   405
Will give you satisfaction, you might have't.

OTHELLO Give me a living reason she's disloyal.

IAGO I do not like the office –
But, sith I am entered in this cause so far,
Pricked to't by foolish honesty and love,   410
I will go on. I lay with Cassio lately,
And being troubled with a raging tooth,
I could not sleep.
There are a kind of men so loose of soul
That in their sleeps will mutter their affairs.   415
One of this kind is Cassio.
In sleep I heard him say, 'Sweet Desdemona,
Let us be wary, let us hide our loves!'
And then, sir, would he gripe and wring my hand,

Iago describes Cassio's dream about Desdemona. He then tells Othello that he has seen Cassio with Desdemona's handkerchief.

425 **but**: only

426 **denoted ... conclusion**: was evidence that something had already happened

427 **'Tis ... doubt**: You're probably right

428 **thicken**: add weight to

433 **Spotted**: embroidered

THINK ABOUT for GCSE

Characterisation

• After telling Othello about Cassio talking in his sleep, Iago seems to play it down when he says 'Nay, this was but his dream' (line 425). What are his possible motives for saying that?

• Having made Othello angry, Iago seems to restrain him (line 430). Why does he do this? Where else has Iago used this technique of leading Othello on, then drawing him back?

Language

• What is Iago suggesting by using the word 'other' in lines 428 and 439?

440 **the slave**: i.e. Cassio

443 **fond**: foolish

446 **hearted**: in the heart

447 **fraught**: burden

448 **aspics'**: asps' (poisonous snakes)

content: patient

	Cry 'O sweet creature!' – and then kiss me hard,	420
	As if he plucked up kisses by the roots	
	That grew upon my lips – then laid his leg	
	Over my thigh, and sighed, and kissed – and then	
	Cried 'Cursèd fate, that gave thee to the Moor!'	

OTHELLO   O monstrous! – monstrous!

IAGO   Nay, this was but his dream.   **425**

OTHELLO   But this denoted a foregone conclusion –

IAGO   'Tis a shrewd doubt, though it be but a dream –
And this may help to thicken other proofs
That do demonstrate thinly.

OTHELLO   I'll tear her all to pieces!

IAGO   Nay – yet be wise. Yet we see nothing done.   **430**
She may be honest yet. Tell me but this:
Have you not sometimes seen a handkerchief
Spotted with strawberries in your wife's hand?

OTHELLO   I gave her such a one – 'twas my first gift.

IAGO   I know not that: but such a handkerchief –   **435**
I am sure it was your wife's – did I today
See Cassio wipe his beard with.

OTHELLO   If it be that –

IAGO   If it be that, or any that was hers,
It speaks against her with the other proofs.

OTHELLO   O, that the slave had forty thousand lives!   **440**
One is too poor, too weak for my revenge.
Now do I see 'tis true. Look here, Iago:
All my fond love thus do I blow to heaven. –
'Tis gone.
Arise, black vengeance, from the hollow hell!   **445**
Yield up, O love, thy crown and hearted throne
To tyrannous hate! Swell, bosom, with thy fraught –
For 'tis of aspics' tongues.

IAGO   Yet be content –

OTHELLO   O, blood, blood, blood!

Othello swears to take bloody revenge. Iago promises to support him and says that he will kill Cassio. Othello makes Iago his lieutenant.

THINK ABOUT for GCSE

Language
- How does the image on lines 451 to 458 help to illustrate the nature of Othello's 'bloody thoughts'?

Characterisation
- Knowing Iago's methods, what would you say about his plea to Othello in line 472?

Structure and form
- In Act 1 Iago talked about 'double knavery' (Act 1 Scene 3, line 385). Which double aim has he achieved by the end of this scene?

Themes and issues
- What has this scene revealed about the nature of **jealousy**, as Shakespeare depicts it?

---

451   **Pontic Sea**: Black Sea (The Romans believed this flowed into the Sea of Marmora but never ebbed back.)
452   **compulsive**: irresistible
453   **feels ... ebb**: never flows back again
454   **Propontic**: Sea of Marmora
       Hellespont: Dardenelles Straits
457   **capable**: all-embracing

458   **marble**: 1 shining; 2 hard (as his determination)
460   **engage**: pledge / promise

462   **clip**: embrace / enclose

464   **execution**: activity / application
       wit: intelligence
466–7   **to obey ... ever**: I will perform whatever bloody deed you command me to do because of the pity I feel for you

469   **to't**: to the test

473   **lewd minx**: lustful creature
474   **apart**: aside / privately
475   **furnish**: equip

IAGO	Patience, I say. Your mind may change.	450

OTHELLO   Never, Iago. – Like to the Pontic Sea,
Whose icy current and compulsive course
Ne'er feels retiring ebb, but keeps due on
To the Propontic and the Hellespont,
Even so my bloody thoughts, with violent pace, 455
Shall ne'er look back, ne'er ebb to humble love,
Till that a capable and wide revenge
Swallow them up.

He kneels.

                    – Now, by yond marble heaven,
In the due reverence of a sacred vow
I here engage my words.

IAGO   Do not rise yet.   460

IAGO *kneels.*

        – Witness, you ever-burning lights above,
You elements that clip us round about,
Witness that here Iago doth give up
The execution of his wit, hands, heart,
To wronged Othello's service. Let him command, 465
And to obey shall be in me remorse,
What bloody business ever.

They rise.

OTHELLO   I greet thy love,
Not with vain thanks but with acceptance bounteous,
And will upon the instant put thee to't.
Within these three days let me hear thee say 470
That Cassio's not alive.

IAGO   My friend is dead.
'Tis done at your request. But let *her* live.

OTHELLO   Damn her, lewd minx! O, damn her! – damn her!
Come, go with me apart. I will withdraw
To furnish me with some swift means of death 475
For the fair devil. Now art thou my lieutenant.

IAGO   I am your own for ever.

                                 Exeunt.

In this scene ...

- When Desdemona pleads with Othello to take Cassio back, he demands to see her handkerchief and is angry when she cannot produce it. Emilia suspects that Othello is jealous.
- Bianca complains that Cassio has been avoiding her, but agrees to copy the embroidery from the handkerchief he has found.

Desdemona asks the Clown to find Cassio and tells Emilia how anxious she is at having lost her handkerchief.

1   **sirrah**: a term of address used for servants
    lies: is lodging

4–5   **for ... stabbing**: any soldier would stab a person for calling him a liar

6   **Go to**: Oh come on

7   **is ... lie**: would be to tell you I am lying

10–11   **lie ... throat**: tell a bare-faced lie

12   **be edified**: learn

13   **catechize**: go through a question-and-answer routine with

16   **moved**: attempted to persuade

17   **compass**: reach
    wit: intelligence

22   **crusadoes**: gold coins
    but: if it were not that
24   **were**: would be

THINK ABOUT for GCSE

Structure and form

- What are the purposes of this exchange between Desdemona and the Clown? For example, think about the mood of the long scene which has just finished, the play on the word 'lies' (lines 1 to 11), and the way in which simple ideas are hidden by complicated language (lines 12 to 13).

Characterisation

- If Emilia is Desdemona's friend, why doesn't she tell her where the handkerchief is (line 20)?

A courtyard in the fortress.

Enter DESDEMONA *and* EMILIA, *with* CLOWN.

DESDEMONA	Do you know, sirrah, where Lieutenant Cassio lies?
CLOWN	I dare not say he lies anywhere.
DESDEMONA	Why, man?
CLOWN	He's a soldier, and for one to say a soldier lies is stabbing.

5

DESDEMONA	Go to. Where lodges he?
CLOWN	To tell you where he lodges is to tell you where I lie.
DESDEMONA	Can anything be made of this?
CLOWN	I know not where he lodges – and for me to devise a lodging, and say he lies here or he lies there, were to lie in mine own throat.

10

DESDEMONA	Can you enquire him out, and be edified by report?
CLOWN	I will catechize the world for him: that is, make questions, and by them answer.
DESDEMONA	Seek him: bid him come hither. Tell him I have moved my lord on his behalf and hope all will be well.

15

CLOWN	To do this is within the compass of man's wit, and therefore I will attempt the doing of it.

Exit CLOWN.

DESDEMONA	Where should I lose the handkerchief, Emilia?
EMILIA	I know not, madam.

20

DESDEMONA	Believe me, I had rather lose my purse Full of crusadoes. And but my noble Moor Is true of mind, and made of no such baseness As jealous creatures are, it were enough To put him to ill thinking.

When Desdemona asks Othello to see Cassio, he asks for her handkerchief.

27 **humours**: jealous moods

30 **dissemble**: deceive / pretend

32 **moist**: Some people believed that a hot and moist palm was a sign of a passionate and lustful nature.
34 **argues**: is a sign of
fruitfulness: 1 generosity; 2 fertility
liberal: 1 generous; 2 lustful
36 **sequester**: restraint
37 **castigation**: harsh discipline
exercise devout: regular prayers
40 **frank**: 1 open; 2 revealing; 3 too free

42 **The hearts … hands**: In the old days people gave their hearts in marriage when they gave their hands
43 **our new heraldry**: i.e. the new way of behaving (He imagines emblems on a coat of arms.)
45 **chuck**: a term of affection
47 **salt … rheum**: nasty running cold

THINK ABOUT for GCSE

Context
• How does Othello use the Early Modern belief that a moist palm was a sign of a hot and passionate nature (lines 33 to 40)?

Language
• In an aside (line 30) Othello tells us how hard it is to keep up the pretence with Desdemona that all is well. In what ways does he use words with double meanings to help him to say what he is really thinking without her understanding him? Look at lines 34 to 43.

EMILIA	Is he not jealous?	25

DESDEMONA Who, he? I think the sun where he was born
Drew all such humours from him.

Enter OTHELLO.

EMILIA Look where he comes.

DESDEMONA I will not leave him now till Cassio
Be called to him. – How is't with you, my lord?

OTHELLO Well, my good lady. – (*Aside*) O, hardness to dissemble! – 30
How do you, Desdemona?

DESDEMONA Well, my good lord.

OTHELLO Give me your hand. This hand is moist, my lady.

DESDEMONA It yet hath felt no age, nor known no sorrow.

OTHELLO This argues fruitfulness and liberal heart.
Hot – hot and moist. This hand of yours requires 35
A sequester from liberty, fasting and prayer,
Much castigation, exercise devout –
For here's a young and sweating devil here
That commonly rebels. 'Tis a good hand,
A frank one.

DESDEMONA You may, indeed, say so – 40
For 'twas that hand that gave away my heart.

OTHELLO A liberal hand! The hearts of old gave hands,
But our new heraldry is hands, not hearts.

DESDEMONA I cannot speak of this. Come now, your promise

OTHELLO What promise, chuck? 45

DESDEMONA I have sent to bid Cassio come speak with you.

OTHELLO I have a salt and sorry rheum offends me. –
Lend me thy handkerchief.

DESDEMONA Here, my lord.

OTHELLO That which I gave you.

DESDEMONA I have it not about me.

145

Othello tells Desdemona that
the handkerchief has magical
powers. She denies that she has
lost it.

53 **charmer**: enchantress / witch

55 **amiable**: lovable

57–8 **my father's ... loathèd**: she would
        become hateful to my father
58 **spirits**: emotions
59 **fancies**: loves
60 **wive**: marry
62 **darling**: treasured object
63 **perdition**: damnation

THINK ABOUT for GCSE

Characterisation

• What does Othello's story
  about the handkerchief in
  lines 51 to 71 tell us about
  him? Does he believe the
  story he is telling? What
  effect does he hope it will
  have upon Desdemona?
  Does it have this desired
  effect?

Language

• Some people argue that
  Shakespeare reflects
  Othello's 'foreignness' in
  his unusual references,
  vocabulary and sentence
  structure. How might lines
  66 to 68 support this view?

---

65 **web**: weave
66 **sibyl**: prophetess / fortune-teller
66–7 **that ... compasses**: i.e. who had lived
        for 200 years
68 **prophetic fury**: inspired fit
      work: embroidered pattern
69 **hallowed**: sacred
70 **mummy**: substance from mummified
      bodies
      the skilful: trained people
71 **Conserved of**: made from
73 **would**: I wish

75 **startingly**: disjointedly
      rash: excitedly
76 **out o' the way**: gone astray

79 **an if**: if

OTHELLO	Not?	**50**
DESDEMONA	No, faith, my lord.	
OTHELLO	That's a fault. That handkerchief	

OTHELLO
                    That's a fault. That handkerchief
Did an Egyptian to my mother give.
She was a charmer, and could almost read
The thoughts of people. She told her, while she kept it
'Twould make her amiable and subdue my father   **55**
Entirely to her love. But if she lost it
Or made a gift of it, my father's eye
Should hold her loathèd, and his spirits should hunt
After new fancies. She, dying, gave it me,
And bid me, when my fate would have me wive   **60**
To give it her. I did so – and take heed on't:
Make it a darling like your precious eye.
To lose't or give't away were such perdition
As nothing else could match.

DESDEMONA
                              Is't possible?

OTHELLO
'Tis true. There's magic in the web of it.   **65**
A sibyl that had numbered in the world
The sun to course two hundred compasses,
In her prophetic fury sewed the work.
The worms were hallowed that did breed the silk,
And it was dyed in mummy which the skilful   **70**
Conserved of maidens' hearts.

DESDEMONA
                              Indeed? Is't true?

OTHELLO
Most veritable. Therefore look to't well.

DESDEMONA
Then would to God that I had never seen it!

OTHELLO
Ha! Wherefore?

DESDEMONA
Why do you speak so startingly and rash?   **75**

OTHELLO
Is't lost? Is't gone? Speak! Is it out o' the way?

DESDEMONA
Heaven bless us!

OTHELLO
Say you?

DESDEMONA
It is not lost. But what an if it were?

Desdemona tries to change the subject back to Cassio but Othello demands to see the handkerchief. When she cannot produce it, he storms out. Emilia suspects that he is jealous.

83 **suit**: request

85 **My mind misgives**: I have a bad feeling about this

87 **sufficient**: able

THINK ABOUT for GCSE

Characterisation

* Why doesn't Desdemona answer Othello's request about the handkerchief directly (line 49) and then persist in lying or changing the subject (lines 79 to 84)?

Language

* What examples of Othello's increasing loss of self-control are there here (lines 74 to 92)? Look at the length of his speeches, the disjointed utterances, the mixture of questions, commands and exclamations, and the references to the handkerchief.

Structure and form

* What do you think Iago has been saying to Cassio before they enter? What does Iago mean by 'There is no other way' (line 101)?

89 **love**: friendship for him

91 **to blame**: wrong to treat me like this

92 **Zounds**: By God's wounds (a powerful oath)

95 **wonder**: magic
96 **unhappy**: unlucky

97 **'Tis … man**: Even a year or two won't show us what a man is really like
98 **but**: only

102 **lo, the happiness**: i.e. luckily, here she is
     importune: plead with

Othello	How?	80
Desdemona	I say it is not lost.	
Othello	Fetch it! Let me see't!	
Desdemona	Why, so I can, sir – but I will not now. This is a trick to put me from my suit. Pray you – let Cassio be received again.	
Othello	Fetch me the handkerchief! My mind misgives.	85
Desdemona	Come, come! You'll never meet a more sufficient man –	
Othello	The handkerchief!	
Desdemona	A man that all his time Hath founded his good fortunes on your love, Shared dangers with you –	90
Othello	The handkerchief!	
Desdemona	I' faith, you are to blame.	
Othello	Zounds!	

Exit.

Emilia	Is not this man jealous?
Desdemona	I ne'er saw this before. Sure there's some wonder in this handkerchief – I am most unhappy in the loss of it.
Emilia	'Tis not a year or two shows us a man. They are all but stomachs, and we all but food: They eat us hungerly, and when they are full, They belch us.

Enter Iago, *with* Cassio.

	– Look you, Cassio and my husband.
Iago	There is no other way: 'tis she must do't. (*Seeing* Desdemona) And lo, the happiness! Go and importune her.
Desdemona	How now, good Cassio? What's the news with you?

95

100

Desdemona tells Cassio that she has not been able to plead successfully with Othello, who is in a strange mood. Iago remarks that if he is angry it must be something very serious.

THINK ABOUT for GCSE

Performance and staging

• If you were the director, how would you want Emilia to behave during Othello's interrogation of Desdemona (lines 49 to 92) and afterwards?

Characterisation

• Why is Iago keen to stress that something really important must have happened to make Othello angry (lines 128 to 133)?

104 **beseech**: beg

107 **office**: devoted service

109 **mortal**: deadly serious
110 **nor**: neither
111 **purposed … futurity**: the good things I plan to do in the future
112 **ransom me**: buy my way back
113 **But**: merely
114 **shall … content**: I will force myself to be happy
115 **shut … in**: limit myself to
116 **To fortune's alms**: i.e. and trust to luck
117 **my advocation … tune**: I am having little success at pleading
119 **in favour … altered**: changed as much in his appearance as his mood
120 **So help … sanctified**: I swear by all the blessed spirits
121 **As**: that
122 **stood … displeasure**: have been a target for his anger

130 **his very arm**: right next to him
131 **Puffed**: blasted away
132 **of moment**: extremely urgent and important
133 **There's … indeed**: It must be really serious
134 **of state**: to do with state affairs
135 **unhatched practice**: previously hidden plot
136 **Made demonstrable**: revealed

CASSIO   Madam, my former suit. I do beseech you
                     That by your virtuous means I may again   105
                     Exist, and be a member of his love
                     Whom I, with all the office of my heart,
                     Entirely honour. I would not be delayed.
                     If my offence be of such mortal kind
                     That nor my service past, nor present sorrows,   110
                     Nor purposed merit in futurity,
                     Can ransom me into his love again,
                     But to know so must be my benefit. –
                     So shall I clothe me in a forced content,
                     And shut myself up in some other course   115
                     To fortune's alms.

DESDEMONA   Alas, thrice-gentle Cassio,
                     My advocation is not now in tune.
                     My lord is not my lord – nor should I know him
                     Were he in favour as in humour altered.
                     So help me every spirit sanctified,   120
                     As I have spoken for you all my best,
                     And stood within the blank of his displeasure
                     For my free speech! You must awhile be patient.
                     What I can do I will – and more I will
                     Than for myself I dare. Let that suffice you.   125

IAGO   Is my lord angry?

EMILIA   He went hence but now,
                     And certainly in strange unquietness.

IAGO   Can he be angry? I have seen the cannon
                     When it hath blown his ranks into the air
                     And, like the devil, from his very arm   130
                     Puffed his own brother. And is *he* angry? –
                     Something of moment then. I will go meet him.
                     There's matter in't indeed if he be angry.

DESDEMONA   I prithee do so.

                                               Exit IAGO.

                     – Something sure of state,
                     Either from Venice, or some unhatched practice   135
                     Made demonstrable here in Cyprus to him,

Desdemona believes that
Othello might have been upset
by official messages from
Venice. Emilia still suspects that
he is jealous. As they leave,
Cassio is met by Bianca.

137 **puddled**: muddied
138 **wrangle with**: argue about
139 **object**: real concern
140 **endues**: leads
141 **members**: limbs

143 **look for**: expect
     observancy: affectionate attention
144 **the bridal**: our wedding day
     Beshrew: Curse
145 **unhandsome**: unskilful
146 **Arraigning**: accusing / blaming
147 **suborned**: influenced (to give false
     evidence)
148 **indicted**: charged / accused
149 **conception**: silly idea
150 **toy**: fancy

153 **the cause**: a particular reason
154 **for**: because
155 **Begot**: fathered

THINK ABOUT for GCSE

Relationships

- Some actresses playing
  Emilia have taken the
  view that she has a bad
  relationship with Iago and
  a poor view of men in
  general. What evidence is
  there for this interpretation?
  Look at lines 97 to 100
  and 152 to 155. What
  experience of jealousy
  might she have had? Look
  back at Act 2 Scene 1, lines
  283 to 287.

Characterisation

- How accurate is Emilia's
  description of jealousy as it
  applies to Othello?
- What does this dialogue
  reveal about the contrasts
  between Emilia and
  Desdemona?

159 **fit**: in the right mood

162 **make ... home**: are you doing here

Hath puddled his clear spirit. And in such cases
Men's natures wrangle with inferior things,
Though great ones are their object. 'Tis even so –
For let our finger ache, and it endues   140
Our other, healthful members even to a sense
Of pain. Nay, we must think men are not gods,
Nor of them look for such observancy
As fits the bridal. Beshrew me much, Emilia,
I was, unhandsome warrior as I am,   145
Arraigning his unkindness with my soul –
But now I find I had suborned the witness,
And he's indicted falsely.

EMILIA   Pray heaven it be
State matters, as you think, and no conception
Nor no jealous toy concerning you.   150

DESDEMONA   Alas the day! I never gave him cause.

EMILIA   But jealous souls will not be answered so.
They are not ever jealous for the cause,
But jealous for they're jealous. It is a monster
Begot upon itself, born on itself.   155

DESDEMONA   Heaven keep that monster from Othello's mind!

EMILIA   Lady, amen.

DESDEMONA   I will go seek him. Cassio, walk here about.
If I do find him fit, I'll move your suit
And seek to effect it to my uttermost.   160

CASSIO   I humbly thank your ladyship.

                                    Exit DESDEMONA, *with* EMILIA.

Enter BIANCA.

BIANCA   Save you, friend Cassio!

CASSIO   What make you from home?
How is it with you, my most fair Bianca?
I' faith, sweet love, I was coming to your house.

Bianca accuses Cassio of avoiding her. He asks her to make a copy of the embroidery on the handkerchief he found in his lodgings.

167   **Eight score eight**: Eight twenties, plus eight
168   **dial**: clock

170   **pressed**: weighed down
171   **continuate**: uninterrupted
172   **Strike ... score**: pay off this debt

173   **Take ... out**: make a copy of this embroidery for me

174   **friend**: lover
175   **To ... cause**: I now see the reason for your absence

176   **Go to**: Don't be ridiculous

THINK ABOUT *for* GCSE

Structure and form

- How does Bianca's complaint (lines 166 to 169) help to give the impression that Cassio must have been on Cyprus for a quite some time? Why is it important for the audience to be told this?

Relationships

- What impression do we receive here of the relationship between Bianca and Cassio?

Characterisation

- What does line 181 tell us about Iago's efficiency in putting his plans into practice? Look back at Act 3 Scene 3, lines 319 to 322.

182   **Ere ... demanded**: Before somebody asks for it back

186   **attend here on**: wait here for
187   **no addition**: i.e. it will do me no good
188   **womaned**: accompanied by a woman

190   **bring**: accompany

BIANCA	And I was going to your lodging, Cassio. 165
	What, keep a week away? Seven days and nights?
	Eight score eight hours? And lovers' absent hours
	More tedious than the dial eight score times?
	O weary reckoning!

CASSIO	Pardon me, Bianca.
	I have this while with leaden thoughts been pressed, 170
	But I shall in a more continuate time
	Strike off this score of absence. Sweet Bianca,
	(*Giving her Desdemona's handkerchief*)
	Take me this work out.

BIANCA	O, Cassio, whence came this?
	This is some token from a newer friend!
	To the felt absence now I feel a cause. 175
	Is't come to this? Well, well.

CASSIO	Go to, woman!
	Throw your vile guesses in the devil's teeth,
	From whence you have them. You are jealous now
	That this is from some mistress, some remembrance.
	No, by my faith, Bianca.

BIANCA	Why, whose is it? 180

CASSIO	I know not neither: I found it in my chamber.
	I like the work well. Ere it be demanded,
	As like enough it will, I would have it copied.
	Take it and do't, and leave me for this time.

BIANCA	Leave you? Wherefore? 185

CASSIO	I do attend here on the general
	And think it no addition, nor my wish,
	To have him see me womaned.

BIANCA	Why, I pray you?

CASSIO	Not that I love you not.

BIANCA	But that you do not love me!
	I pray you bring me on the way a little, 190
	And say if I shall see you soon at night.

Cassio promises to see Bianca
again soon.

194 I ... circumstanced: I will have to put
up with the way things are

THINK ABOUT for **GCSE**

Themes and issues
* In what ways does this
  exchange between Bianca
  and Cassio add to our
  understanding of **jealousy**
  in this play?

Cassio   'Tis but a little way that I can bring you,
              For I attend here – but I'll see you soon.

Bianca   'Tis very good: I must be circumstanced.

                                                        Exeunt.

In this scene ...

- At the thought that Desdemona is having an affair, Othello briefly falls down in a trance.
- Iago places Othello where he can watch and hear a conversation with Cassio. Iago questions Cassio about Bianca knowing that Othello will think that Cassio's mocking replies are about Desdemona.
- Bianca enters and produces the handkerchief, convincing Othello that Desdemona is guilty. He decides to kill her. Iago promises to kill Cassio.
- Important orders arrive from Venice, but Othello remains agitated and strikes Desdemona in public.

Determined to drive Othello mad with jealousy, Iago reminds him of the handkerchief.

2 **unauthorized**: 1 forbidden; 2 adulterous

3 **friend**: lover

6 **hypocrisy ... devil**: i.e. an innocent act which appears sinful

7 **do so**: i.e. lie in bed together

8 **they tempt heaven**: i.e. even heavenly powers may not save them

9 **venial slip**: minor sin

THINK ABOUT for GCSE

Structure and form

- Like the opening scene of the play, Act 4 Scene 1 starts in the middle of a conversation. What might Iago and Othello have been saying just before they enter?

Characterisation

- Why does Iago remind Othello about the handkerchief (lines 10 and 18), when it has already served its purpose?

13 **bestow't on**: give it to

16 **essence**: inner quality

17 **have it**: i.e. appear to possess it

22 **Boding to all**: acting as a sign that there is plague within the house

Cyprus: a courtyard in the fortress.

Enter OTHELLO *and* IAGO.

IAGO	Will you think so?
OTHELLO	Think so, Iago?
IAGO	What, To kiss in private?
OTHELLO	An unauthorized kiss!
IAGO	– Or to be naked with her friend in bed An hour or more, not meaning any harm?
OTHELLO	Naked in bed, Iago, and not mean harm? It is hypocrisy against the devil! They that mean virtuously, and yet do so, The devil their virtue tempts, and they tempt heaven.
IAGO	If they do nothing, 'tis a venial slip. But if I give my wife a handkerchief –
OTHELLO	What then?
IAGO	Why, then 'tis hers, my lord – and being hers, She may, I think, bestow't on any man.
OTHELLO	She is protectress of her honour too. May she give that?
IAGO	Her honour is an essence that's not seen: They have it very oft that have it not. But for the handkerchief –
OTHELLO	By heaven, I would most gladly have forgot it! Thou said'st – O, it comes o'er my memory As doth the raven o'er the infected house, Boding to all! – he had my handkerchief.
IAGO	Ay, what of that?
OTHELLO	That's not so good now.

IAGO Will you think so?

OTHELLO Think so, Iago?

IAGO What,
To kiss in private?

OTHELLO An unauthorized kiss!

IAGO – Or to be naked with her friend in bed
An hour or more, not meaning any harm?

OTHELLO Naked in bed, Iago, and not mean harm? 5
It is hypocrisy against the devil!
They that mean virtuously, and yet do so,
The devil their virtue tempts, and they tempt heaven.

IAGO If they do nothing, 'tis a venial slip.
But if I give my wife a handkerchief – 10

OTHELLO What then?

IAGO Why, then 'tis hers, my lord – and being hers,
She may, I think, bestow't on any man.

OTHELLO She is protectress of her honour too.
May she give that? 15

IAGO Her honour is an essence that's not seen:
They have it very oft that have it not.
But for the handkerchief –

OTHELLO By heaven, I would most gladly have forgot it!
Thou said'st – O, it comes o'er my memory 20
As doth the raven o'er the infected house,
Boding to all! – he had my handkerchief.

IAGO Ay, what of that?

OTHELLO That's not so good now.

When Iago claims that Cassio has been boasting about his affair with Desdemona, Othello falls down in a trance.

25 **as knaves ... abroad**: just as there are villains around

26 **importunate suit**: urgent persuasion

27 **voluntary dotage**: willing infatuation

28 **Convincèd**: overcome her reluctance

supplied them: satisfied her sexually

31 **unswear**: deny

THINK ABOUT for GCSE

Language

• Why does Iago play on the word 'lie' (lines 34 to 35)? Think about the word's different meanings and the effect he knows the wordplay will have on Othello.

• How does Othello's language (lines 36 to 44) reflect his mental and physical state? Think about what he says and how he says it.

Performance and staging

• In a performance, what should Othello's 'trance' look like? Look, for example, at lines 40 and 42.

36 **Lie with**: Have sex with

Lie on: 1 Tell lies about 2 Have sex with

37 **belie**: tell lies about

Zounds: God's wounds (a powerful oath)

fulsome: disgusting

40 **Nature**: My nature

invest: dress

41 **shadowing**: darkening

42 **instruction**: basis in fact

46 **credulous**: gullible

47 **chaste dames**: sexually virtuous women

48 **reproach**: scandal and shame

IAGO	What if I had said I'd seen him do you wrong?
	Or heard him say – as knaves be such abroad 25
	Who having by their own importunate suit
	Or voluntary dotage of some mistress,
	Convincèd or supplied them, cannot choose
	But they must blab –
OTHELLO	Hath he said anything?
IAGO	He hath, my lord – but be you well assured, 30
	No more than he'll unswear.
OTHELLO	What hath he said?
IAGO	Why, that he did – I know not what he did.
OTHELLO	What? What?
IAGO	Lie –
OTHELLO	With her?
IAGO	With her, on her – what you will. 35
OTHELLO	Lie with her? Lie on her? – We say lie on her when they belie her. – Lie with her! Zounds, that's fulsome! – Handkerchief – confessions – handkerchief! To confess, and be hanged for his labour – first to be hanged, and then to confess! I tremble at it. Nature would not invest 40 herself in such shadowing passion without some instruction. It is not words that shakes me thus. – Pish! Noses, ears, and lips! Is't possible? – Confess? – Handkerchief? – O devil!

He falls down in a trance.

IAGO	Work on, my medicine – work! 45
	Thus credulous fools are caught –
	And many worthy and chaste dames even thus,
	All guiltless, meet reproach. What ho! My lord!
	My lord, I say! Othello!

Enter CASSIO.

	How now – Cassio!
CASSIO	What's the matter? 50

Iago tells Othello that Cassio has been present while he was unconscious. He reminds Othello that many men have unfaithful wives.

51 **is fallen … epilepsy**: has had a seizure

53 **forbear**: don't
54 **lethargy**: fit of unconsciousness
    have … course: be allowed to pass naturally

58 **straight**: straight away
59 **great occasion**: an important matter

61 **mock me**: Othello believes that Iago is referring to his cuckold's horns.

62 **Would**: I wish

65 **civil**: civilised

THINK ABOUT *for* GCSE

Characterisation

• Why might Othello think that Iago is mocking him (line 61)? Do you think he really is mocking him?

• Iago's puzzling comment (lines 73 to 74) could mean either: (a) 'No. If I am a cuckold, I want to know. Then I will know how to treat my wife'; or (b) 'No. I want to know. Knowing that I am imperfect, I know she is bound to be imperfect too'. Which do you think is more likely?

67–8 **Think … you**: i.e. Remember that every married man is in the same situation
69 **unproper**: shared (i.e. with their wife's lover)
70 **peculiar**: exclusively theirs
71 **arch-mock**: greatest mock
72 **lip a wanton**: kiss an immoral woman
    in a secure couch: i.e. without suspecting she is unfaithful

76 **Confine … list**: i.e. keep your self-control

| IAGO | My lord is fallen into an epilepsy. |
| | This is his second fit – he had one yesterday. |

| CASSIO | Rub him about the temples. |

| IAGO | No – forbear. |

The lethargy must have his quiet course.
If not, he foams at mouth, and by and by   **55**
Breaks out to savage madness. Look, he stirs.
Do you withdraw yourself a little while.
He will recover straight. When he is gone,
I would on great occasion speak with you.

Exit CASSIO.

– How is it, general? Have you not hurt your head?   **60**

| OTHELLO | Dost thou mock me? |

| IAGO | I mock you? No, by heaven! |

Would you would bear your fortune like a man!

| OTHELLO | A hornèd man's a monster and a beast. |

| IAGO | There's many a beast then in a populous city, |
| | And many a civil monster.   **65** |

| OTHELLO | Did he confess it? |

| IAGO | Good sir, be a man. |

Think every bearded fellow that's but yoked
May draw with you. There's millions now alive
That nightly lie in those unproper beds
Which they dare swear peculiar. Your case is better.   **70**
O, 'tis the spite of hell, the fiend's arch-mock,
To lip a wanton in a secure couch,
And to suppose her chaste! No, let me know –
And knowing what I am, I know what *she* shall be.

| OTHELLO | O, thou art wise. 'Tis certain. |

| IAGO | Stand you awhile apart: **75** |

Confine yourself but in a patient list.
Whilst you were here, o'erwhelmèd with your grief –
A passion most unsuiting such a man –
Cassio came hither. I shifted him away

Iago persuades Othello to hide and watch his conversation with Cassio. Iago begins to question Cassio about Bianca, knowing that Othello will think Cassio is boasting about his affair with Desdemona.

80 **laid … ecstasy**: used your seizure as the obvious excuse

82 **encave**: hide

83 **fleers**: sneers
    gibes: insults
    notable scorns: blatant mockery

87 **cope**: have sex with

88 **mark his gesture**: watch what he does

89 **all in … spleen**: entirely ruled by your temper

92 **not amiss**: i.e. the right way to react

THINK ABOUT for GCSE

Language

• Nearly every word in lines 86 to 87 is a monosyllable. How might this help the actor to get the meaning across?

Performance and staging

• Where might Othello conceal himself on the stage of Shakespeare's Globe at line 93 so that he can still see Iago and Cassio? And where could their conversation take place?

Themes and issues

• What might Iago mean by calling Othello's **jealousy** 'unbookish' (line 102)?

95 **housewife**: i.e. prostitute

97 **strumpet's**: whore's

98 **beguile**: deceive

102 **unbookish**: ignorant
    conster: interpret

103 **light**: joking

105 **addition**: title (of lieutenant)

106 **want**: lack

107 **Ply**: Work on

108 **suit**: request

109 **speed**: succeed

	And laid good 'scuse upon your ecstasy;	80
	Bade him anon return, and here speak with me –	
	The which he promised. Do but encave yourself,	
	And mark the fleers, the gibes, and notable scorns	
	That dwell in every region of his face.	
	For I will make him tell the tale anew:	85
	Where, how, how oft, how long ago, and when	
	He hath, and is again to cope your wife.	
	I say but mark his gesture. Marry, patience! –	
	Or I shall say you're all in all in spleen,	
	And nothing of a man.	

OTHELLO   Dost thou hear, Iago?   90
I will be found most cunning in my patience;
But – dost thou hear? – most bloody.

IAGO   That's not amiss –
But yet keep time in all. Will you withdraw?

OTHELLO *moves aside, and hides where he can watch but
cannot hear.*

(*Aside*) Now will I question Cassio of Bianca,
A housewife that by selling her desires   95
Buys herself bread and cloth. It is a creature
That dotes on Cassio (as 'tis the strumpet's plague
To beguile many and be beguiled by one).
He, when he hears of her, cannot refrain
From the excess of laughter.

Enter CASSIO.

                              – Here he comes.   100
As he shall smile, Othello shall go mad –
And his unbookish jealousy must conster
Poor Cassio's smiles, gestures, and light behaviours
Quite in the wrong. – How do you, lieutenant?

CASSIO   The worser that you give me the addition   105
Whose want even kills me.

IAGO   Ply Desdemona well, and you are sure on't.
Now, if this suit lay in Bianca's power,
How quickly should you speed!

Iago's plan works: the more Cassio laughs about Bianca, the more Othello thinks he is talking about his relationship with Desdemona.

109 caitiff: wretch

113 faintly: without meaning it
out: off

114 importunes: begs / persuades
115 Go ... said: Oh yes, well done

119 triumph: gloat
Roman: i.e. conqueror
120 customer: prostitute
120–1 I prithee ... wit: Please, give me credit for some intelligence
121 unwholesome: unhealthy
123 They ... win: i.e. But I'll have the last laugh
124 cry: rumour

127 scored: wounded

128 giving out: report
129 out of ... flattery: i.e. she is flattering herself

THINK ABOUT for GCSE

Performance and staging
- The stage direction at line 131 says that Othello moves closer. On the stage of Shakespeare's Globe, where could he go so that he would still be concealed?
- What actions should the actor playing Cassio perform as he tells Iago of his meeting with Bianca (lines 132 to 139)?

Structure and form
- How do lines 52 and 133 help to give the impression that the characters have been on Cyprus for more than just a day?

132 even now: a moment ago

134 bauble: worthless plaything

137 imports: shows / suggests

CASSIO	Alas, poor caitiff!
OTHELLO	(*Aside*) Look how he laughs already! **110**
IAGO	I never knew a woman love man so.
CASSIO	Alas, poor rogue! I think, i' faith, she loves me.
OTHELLO	(*Aside*) Now he denies it faintly, and laughs it out.
IAGO	Do you hear, Cassio?
OTHELLO	(*Aside*) Now he importunes him To tell it o'er. Go to – well said, well said! **115**
IAGO	She gives it out that you shall marry her. Do you intend it?
CASSIO	Ha, ha, ha!
OTHELLO	(*Aside*) Do you triumph, Roman? Do you triumph?
CASSIO	I marry her? What! – a customer? I prithee bear some **120** charity to my wit. Do not think it so unwholesome. Ha, ha, ha!
OTHELLO	(*Aside*) So, so, so, so. They laugh that win.
IAGO	Faith, the cry goes that you shall marry her.
CASSIO	Prithee, say true. **125**
IAGO	I am a very villain else!
OTHELLO	(*Aside*) Have you scored me? Well.
CASSIO	This is the monkey's own giving out! She is persuaded I will marry her out of her own love and flattery, not out of my promise. **130**
OTHELLO	(*Aside*) Iago beckons me. Now he begins the story.

OTHELLO *moves quietly closer, to hear.*

CASSIO	She was here even now. She haunts me in every place. I was the other day talking on the sea-bank with certain Venetians, and thither comes the bauble, and falls me thus about my neck – **135**
OTHELLO	(*Aside*) Crying 'O dear Cassio!' as it were. His gesture imports it.

Unexpectedly, Bianca arrives on the scene and angrily brings out the handkerchief, accusing Cassio of accepting it as a token from another girlfriend.

138 hales: drags

144 Before me: an expression of surprise

145 fitchew: 1 polecat; 2 prostitute

147 dam: mother

149–50 take out the work: copy the embroidery

152 minx's token: love-token from a prostitute or mistress
153 hobby-horse: i.e. whore

155 How now: What's the matter

156 should be: looks like

158 prepared for: i.e. never

160 rail: kick up a fuss

163 very fain: very much like to

THINK ABOUT for GCSE

Themes and issues
- **Gender**: What language does Cassio use here to label Bianca a prostitute (look at lines 120 and 145)?
- What is there in her behaviour here that suggests that she is not a prostitute, and that she is in love with Cassio?

Structure and form
- Why is Iago so keen that Cassio should run after Bianca (line 159)?

CASSIO	So hangs, and lolls and weeps upon me – so hales and pulls me! Ha, ha, ha!
OTHELLO	(*Aside*) Now he tells how she plucked him to my chamber. O, I see that nose of yours, but not that dog I shall throw it to!
CASSIO	Well, I must leave her company.
IAGO	Before me! Look where she comes.

Enter BIANCA.

CASSIO	'Tis such another fitchew! – marry, a perfumed one! What do you mean by this haunting of me?
BIANCA	Let the devil and his dam haunt you! What did you mean by that same handkerchief you gave me even now? I was a fine fool to take it. I must take out the work? A likely piece of work, that you should find it in your chamber and know not who left it there! This is some minx's token, and I must take out the work? There! (*She throws the handkerchief at* CASSIO, *who picks it up.*) – Give it your hobby-horse, wheresoever you had it. I'll take out no work on't.
CASSIO	How now, my sweet Bianca? How now? – how now?
OTHELLO	(*Aside*) By heaven, that should be my handkerchief!
BIANCA	If you'll come to supper tonight, you may. If you will not, come when you are next prepared for.

Exit.

IAGO	After her, after her!
CASSIO	Faith, I must. She'll rail in the streets else.
IAGO	Will you sup there?
CASSIO	Yes, I intend so.
IAGO	Well, I may chance to see you, for I would very fain speak with you.
CASSIO	Prithee come. Will you?

140

145

150

155

160

165

Seeing the handkerchief and listening to Cassio have finally convinced Othello that Desdemona and Cassio are having an affair. He resolves to kill Desdemona, although he still loves her.

166 Go to: All right

172 by this hand: i.e. I swear

175 a-killing: being killed

THINK ABOUT for GCSE

Language

• What is the double meaning in Iago's 'by this hand' (line 172)? What might be the effect of the wordplay here?

Characterisation

• Iago could not have known that Bianca would arrive and bring out the handkerchief. How does he show his quick thinking in exploiting the moment here?

• Othello is torn between his love for Desdemona and his jealous fury. How does Iago steer Othello away from affectionate thoughts about her?

183 your way: the way you should be thinking

187 invention: imagination

190 gentle a condition: good-natured

191 *too* gentle: i.e. she gives in too easily

194 fond: foolishly loving
iniquity: sinfulness
give her patent: allow

195 comes near: affects

196 messes: pieces of meat

IAGO	Go to, say no more.

Exit CASSIO.

OTHELLO	(*Coming forward*) How shall I murder him, Iago?	
IAGO	Did you perceive how he laughed at his vice?	
OTHELLO	O Iago!	
IAGO	And did you see the handkerchief?	**170**
OTHELLO	Was that mine?	
IAGO	Yours, by this hand. And to see how he prizes the foolish woman your wife! She gave it him, and he hath given it his whore.	
OTHELLO	I would have him nine years a-killing! – A fine woman, a fair woman, a sweet woman!	**175**
IAGO	Nay, you must forget that.	
OTHELLO	Ay, let her rot, and perish, and be damned tonight! – for she shall not live. No, my heart is turned to stone: I strike it, and it hurts my hand. O, the world hath not a sweeter creature! She might lie by an emperor's side and command him tasks.	**180**
IAGO	Nay, that's not your way.	
OTHELLO	Hang her! I do but say what she is. So delicate with her needle. An admirable musician. O, she will sing the savageness out of a bear! Of so high and plenteous wit and invention –	**185**
IAGO	She's the worse for all this.	
OTHELLO	O, a thousand, a thousand times. – And then, of so gentle a condition!	**190**
IAGO	Ay, *too* gentle.	
OTHELLO	Nay, that's certain. But yet the pity of it, Iago! – O, Iago – the pity of it, Iago.	
IAGO	If you are so fond over her iniquity, give her patent to offend – for if it touch not you, it comes near nobody.	**195**
OTHELLO	I will chop her into messes! Cuckold me!	

On Iago's advice Othello
decides to strangle Desdemona
that night. Iago volunteers
to kill Cassio. Lodovico and
Desdemona arrive with a letter
from Venice.

201 **expostulate**: argue at length
202 **unprovide my mind**: weaken my
determination

206 **be his undertaker**: 1 deal with him;
2 kill him

THINK ABOUT for GCSE

Characterisation
- Why do you think Iago
  wants Othello to strangle
  Desdemona rather than
  poison her (lines 203
  to 204)?

Structure and form
- Iago offers to be Cassio's
  'undertaker' and promises
  'You shall hear more by
  midnight' (lines 206 to
  207). Where earlier did we
  see Iago setting up Cassio's
  murder for that night? Look
  back at page 185.

213 **the instrument ... pleasures**: the letter
which expresses their wishes

IAGO	O, 'tis foul in her.
OTHELLO	With mine officer!
IAGO	That's fouler.
OTHELLO	Get me some poison, Iago, this night. I'll not **200** expostulate with her, lest her body and beauty unprovide my mind again. This night, Iago!
IAGO	Do it not with poison. Strangle her in her bed, even the bed she hath contaminated.
OTHELLO	Good, good. The justice of it pleases. Very good! **205**
IAGO	And for Cassio, let me be his undertaker. You shall hear more by midnight.
OTHELLO	Excellent good!

A trumpet-call is heard.

         – What trumpet is that same?

IAGO	I warrant, something from Venice.

Enter LODOVICO *and* DESDEMONA, *with attendants.*

        'Tis Lodovico –
This comes from the Duke. See, your wife's with him.   **210**

LODOVICO	God save you, worthy general!
OTHELLO	With all my heart, sir.
LODOVICO	The Duke and the senators of Venice greet you.

He gives OTHELLO *a letter.*

OTHELLO	I kiss the instrument of their pleasures.

He opens the letter and reads it.

DESDEMONA	And what's the news, good cousin Lodovico?
IAGO	I am very glad to see you, signior. **215** Welcome to Cyprus.
LODOVICO	I thank you. How does Lieutenant Cassio?
IAGO	Lives, sir.

As Othello reads the letter, he is also listening to Desdemona talking to Lodovico about Cassio. This makes Othello so angry that he strikes her.

219   unkind breach: rift / uncharacteristic disagreement

223   in the paper: reading the letter

226   atone them: bring them together

230   Deputing ... government: replacing him as governor with Cassio

231   By my troth: Believe me
on't: of it

THINK ABOUT for GCSE

Language
- What do you notice about the structure of lines 227 and 231? How might they be performed?

Performance and staging
- If you were the director, how would you stage this part of the scene (lines 209 to 253)? Think about the positions and movement of the actors and the way they would perform their lines.

236   very much: outrageous

ACT 4 SCENE 2

Inside the fortress.

Enter OTHELLO, *with* EMILIA.

OTHELLO	You have seen nothing then?
EMILIA	Nor ever heard, nor ever did suspect.
OTHELLO	Yes: you have seen Cassio and she together.
EMILIA	But then I saw no harm, and then I heard
	Each syllable that breath made up between them.

5

OTHELLO	What – did they never whisper?
EMILIA	Never, my lord.
OTHELLO	Nor send you out o' the way?
EMILIA	Never.
OTHELLO	To fetch her fan, her gloves, her mask, nor nothing?
EMILIA	Never, my lord.
OTHELLO	That's strange.

10

EMILIA	I durst, my lord, to wager she is honest,
	Lay down my soul at stake. If you think other,
	Remove your thought. It doth abuse your bosom.
	If any wretch have put this in your head,
	Let heaven requite it with the serpent's curse!

15

	For if she be not honest, chaste, and true,
	There's no man happy. The purest of their wives
	Is foul as slander.
OTHELLO	Bid her come hither. Go!

Exit EMILIA.

She says enough – yet she's a simple bawd
That cannot say as much. This is a subtle whore,   20
A closet lock and key of villainous secrets –
And yet she'll kneel and pray. I have seen her do it.

Despite Desdemona's insistence that she is a true and loyal wife, Othello accuses her of being unfaithful.

23 chuck: term of affection

25 fancy: fantasy / whim

26 Some of your function: i.e. Do your job (as a brothel-keeper)

27 procreants: people having sex

28 cry 'hem': clear your throat

29 mystery: trade (of brothel-keeper)
   dispatch: hurry up

30 import: mean

THINK ABOUT for GCSE

Context

• Brothels and their bawds (the women who ran them) were often featured in Early Modern plays. What point is Othello making when addressing Emilia (lines 26 to 29)?

Performance and staging

• At the end of Act 3 Scene 3 there is a powerful moment on stage, as both Iago and Othello kneel and swear oaths. Which moments in this scene so far (lines 23 to 46) give the actors the opportunity to create some equally powerful pictures on stage? Look, for example, at lines 24 to 25, line 30 and lines 39 to 40.

35 being … heaven: because you look like an angel

36 double-damned: i.e. through being a whore and denying it on oath

41 heavy: unhappy

42 motive of: reason for

43 haply: perhaps

44 An instrument: the person responsible (for having Othello called back to Venice)

Re-enter EMILIA, *with* DESDEMONA.

DESDEMONA	My lord, what is your will?
OTHELLO	Pray, chuck, come hither.
DESDEMONA	What is your pleasure?
OTHELLO	Let me see your eyes.
	Look in my face.
DESDEMONA	What horrible fancy's this?	25

OTHELLO   (*To* EMILIA) Some of your function, mistress:
Leave procreants alone and shut the door;
Cough or cry 'hem' if anybody come.
Your mystery, your mystery! – Nay, dispatch!

Exit EMILIA.

DESDEMONA   (*Kneeling*) Upon my knees, what doth your speech
    import?   30
I understand a fury in your words,
But not the words.

OTHELLO   Why? – what art thou?

DESDEMONA   Your wife, my lord – your true and loyal wife.

OTHELLO   Come – swear it! Damn thyself –
Lest, being like one of heaven, the devils themselves   35
Should fear to seize thee. Therefore be double-damned:
Swear thou art honest!

DESDEMONA   Heaven doth truly know it.

OTHELLO   Heaven truly knows that thou art false as hell.

DESDEMONA   To whom, my lord? – With whom? How am I false?

OTHELLO   Ah, Desdemona! Away! Away! Away!   40

DESDEMONA   Alas the heavy day! Why do you weep?
Am I the motive of these tears, my lord?
If haply you my father do suspect
An instrument of this your calling back,
Lay not your blame on me. If you have lost him,   45
I have lost him too.

Othello grieves over Desdemona's unfaithfulness and calls her a whore.

49 Steeped: submerged

53 The fixèd … scorn: i.e. an everlasting figure of fun

56 garnered: stored / harvested

58 fountain: spring

60 cistern: waste-water tank
61 knot and gender: writhe and have sex
Turn … there: Turn pale at the sight of that
62 cherubin: angel
64 esteems me honest: considers me faithful
65 shambles: slaughter-house
66 quicken … blowing: come to life as soon as the eggs are laid
68 would: I wish

69 ignorant: unintentional

72 commoner: prostitute
73 forges: blacksmiths' fires

76 stops: closes up
winks: shuts its eyes (The moon was a symbol of chastity.)
77 bawdy: sexually free
78 mine: cave
80 strumpet: whore

THINK ABOUT for GCSE

Themes and issues
- Othello sees himself as a number on a clock face, pointed at by the hour hand (lines 52 to 54). What idea does this image help to get across? How does it contribute to the theme of **reputation and honour**?

Language
- Look at lines 58 to 61, 66 to 68 and 70 to 71. What is Othello saying about Desdemona? How effective are the images he uses to describe her here?

OTHELLO	Had it pleased heaven
	To try me with affliction – had they rained
	All kinds of sores and shames on my bare head,
	Steeped me in poverty to the very lips,
	Given to captivity me and my utmost hopes,	50
	I should have found in some place of my soul
	A drop of patience. But alas, to make me
	The fixèd figure for the time of scorn
	To point his slow unmoving finger at!
	Yet could I bear that too, well – very well.	55
	But there where I have garnered up my heart,
	Where either I must live or bear no life,
	The fountain from the which my current runs
	Or else dries up – to be discarded thence,
	Or keep it as a cistern for foul toads	60
	To knot and gender in! – Turn thy complexion there,
	Patience, thou young and rose-lipped cherubin!
	Ay – there look grim as hell!

DESDEMONA   I hope my noble lord esteems me honest.

OTHELLO   O ay – as summer flies are in the shambles,   65
             That quicken even with blowing. O thou weed,
             Who art so lovely fair, and smell'st so sweet
             That the sense aches at thee – would thou hadst ne'er
                 been born!

DESDEMONA   Alas! What ignorant sin have I committed?

OTHELLO   Was this fair paper, this most goodly book,   70
             Made to write 'whore' upon? What committed?
             Committed! – O thou public commoner! –
             I should make very forges of my cheeks
             That would to cinders burn up modesty,
             Did I but speak thy deeds. What committed!   75
             Heaven stops the nose at it, and the moon winks;
             The bawdy wind that kisses all it meets
             Is hushed within the hollow mine of earth
             And will not hear it. – What committed!
             Impudent strumpet!

DESDEMONA   By heaven, you do me wrong!   80

OTHELLO   Are not you a strumpet?

Othello storms out, still treating Desdemona as if she were a prostitute. Emilia tries to comfort Desdemona, who is stunned by Othello's behaviour.

82   **this vessel**: my body

87   **cry you mercy**: beg your pardon

90   **office ... Saint Peter**: i.e. guarding the gates of hell (not heaven)

92   **done our course**: finished our business (i.e. having sex)

93   **counsel**: secrets

94   **conceive**: imagine

96   **half asleep**: dazed / stunned

THINK ABOUT for GCSE

Language
- In what ways does Othello's language here continue the theme he started in lines 26 and 29?

Characterisation
- How would you describe Desdemona's reaction to Othello's accusations here? What do you think of her response?

103   **go by water**: be expressed through tears

DESDEMONA	No, as I am a Christian!
	If to preserve this vessel for my lord
	From any other foul unlawful touch
	Be not to be a strumpet, I am none.
OTHELLO	What, not a whore?
DESDEMONA	No, as I shall be saved!

85

OTHELLO	Is't possible?
DESDEMONA	O heaven forgive us!
OTHELLO	I cry you mercy then.
	I took you for that cunning whore of Venice
	That married with Othello. (*Calling* EMILIA) You, mistress –

Enter EMILIA.

That have the office opposite to Saint Peter   90
And keep the gate of hell! You, you, ay, you!
We have done our course. There's money for your pains.

He flings her some coins.

I pray you turn the key and keep our counsel.

Exit.

EMILIA	Alas, what does this gentleman conceive?
	How do you, madam? How do you, my good lady? 95
DESDEMONA	Faith, half asleep.
EMILIA	Good madam, what's the matter with my lord?
DESDEMONA	With who?
EMILIA	Why – with my lord, madam.
DESDEMONA	Who is thy lord?
EMILIA	He that is yours, sweet lady. 100
DESDEMONA	I have none. Do not talk to me, Emilia.
	I cannot weep, nor answers have I none
	But what should go by water. Prithee tonight
	Lay on my bed my wedding sheets, remember. –
	And call thy husband hither.

Iago enters and Emilia tells him that Othello has accused Desdemona of being a whore.

106 meet: fitting

107–8 stick ... opinion: have the slightest reason to criticise

108 least misuse: most insignificant fault

112 chid: scolded

113 am a child to: have no experience of

114 be-whored: called her 'whore'

115 despite: insults

THINK ABOUT *for* **GCSE**

Characterisation

- What contrasts can you see here between Desdemona and Emilia? Look, for example, at their language in lines 117 to 120.

Themes and issues

- **Truth and deception**: How does this part of the scene show Iago's ability to fool people completely? Look particularly at his words to Desdemona and her replies.

---

120 laid such terms: used such language
callet: slut / prostitute

124 forsook: turned her back on

127 Beshrew: Curse
128 trick: strange behaviour

EMILIA	Here's a change indeed!	105

Exit.

DESDEMONA   'Tis meet I should be used so, very meet.
How have I been behaved, that he might stick
The small'st opinion on my least misuse?

Re-enter EMILIA, *with* IAGO.

IAGO   What is your pleasure, madam? How is't with you?

DESDEMONA   I cannot tell. Those that do teach young babes   110
Do it with gentle means and easy tasks.
He might have chid *me* so – for, in good faith,
I am a child to chiding.

IAGO   What is the matter, lady?

EMILIA   Alas, Iago, my lord hath so be-whored her,
Thrown such despite and heavy terms upon her   115
As true hearts cannot bear.

DESDEMONA   Am I that name, Iago?

IAGO   What name, fair lady?

DESDEMONA   Such as she said my lord did say I was.

EMILIA   He called her whore. A beggar in his drink
Could not have laid such terms upon his callet!   120

IAGO   Why did he so?

DESDEMONA   I do not know. I am sure I am none such.

IAGO   Do not weep, do not weep. Alas the day!

EMILIA   Hath she forsook so many noble matches,
Her father and her country, and her friends,   125
To be called whore? Would it not make one weep?

DESDEMONA   It is my wretched fortune.

IAGO   Beshrew him for't!
How comes this trick upon him?

DESDEMONA   Nay, heaven doth know.

Emilia suspects that somebody wicked must have poisoned Othello's mind. Desdemona expresses her love for Othello and asks for Iago's help to win him back.

THINK ABOUT
for GCSE

Characterisation

• Emilia earlier cursed the 'wretch' who might have put ideas into Othello's head (lines 14 to 15). Where does she come even closer to realising the truth in this part of the scene? What prevents her from realising that Iago is responsible?

• Which lines show that Iago has himself been jealous and accused Emilia previously? What did he accuse her of doing?

130 **busy**: interfering
insinuating: wheedling / worming his way into favour

131 **cogging**: deceiving
cozening: cheating
office: job

135 **halter**: hangman's noose

139 **scurvy**: bad / worthless

140 **O heaven … unfold**: I pray heaven expose crooks like that

143 **within door**: more quietly / less publicly

145 **wit**: common sense
the seamy side without: wrong side out

146 **suspect me**: i.e. of adultery

147 **Go to**: i.e. Be quiet

152 **discourse of thought**: my thoughts

153 **that**: if

155 **yet**: still

158 **forswear**: abandon
Unkindness: (can also mean unnatural behaviour)

159 **defeat**: destroy

160 **taint**: spoil

161 **abhor**: revolt

162 **addition**: title (of 'whore')

163 **vanity**: foolish luxury

190

EMILIA	I will be hanged if some eternal villain,	
	Some busy and insinuating rogue,	130
	Some cogging, cozening slave, to get some office,	
	Have not devised this slander. – I'll be hanged else!	

| IAGO | Fie, there is no such man! It is impossible. |

| DESDEMONA | If any such there be, heaven pardon him. |

EMILIA	A halter pardon him! And hell gnaw his bones!	135
	Why should he call her whore? Who keeps her	
	company?	
	What place? What time? What form? What likelihood?	
	The Moor's abused by some most villainous knave,	
	Some base notorious knave, some scurvy fellow.	
	O heaven, that such companions thou'dst unfold,	140
	And put in every honest hand a whip	
	To lash the rascals naked through the world	
	Even from the east to the west!	

| IAGO | Speak within door. |

EMILIA	O fie upon them! Some such squire he was	
	That turned *your* wit the seamy side without	145
	And made you to suspect me with the Moor.	

| IAGO | You are a fool! Go to. |

DESDEMONA	Alas, Iago,	
	What shall I do to win my lord again?	
	Good friend, go to him – for, by this light of heaven,	
	I know not how I lost him. Here I kneel:	150
	If e'er my will did trespass 'gainst his love	
	Either in discourse of thought or actual deed,	
	Or that mine eyes, mine ears, or any sense	
	Delighted them in any other form –	
	Or that I do not yet, and ever did,	155
	And ever will (though he do shake me off	
	To beggarly divorcement) love him dearly,	
	Comfort forswear me! Unkindness may do much,	
	And his unkindness may defeat my life,	
	But never taint my love. I cannot say 'whore'.	160
	It does abhor me now I speak the word.	
	To do the act that might the addition earn	
	Not the world's mass of vanity could make me.	

Roderigo angrily complains to Iago that he has been leading him on and not giving him any real help in his attempt to win Desdemona.

164   **humour**: mood

165   **does him offence**: is annoying him

166   **does chide with**: is taking it out on

167   **If ... other**: If only it were nothing more than that
      but ... warrant: nothing more, I promise you

169   **stay the meat**: wait for their meal

172   **justly**: fairly

173   **What ... contrary**: in what way unfairly

174   **thou ... device**: you fob me off with some excuse

175–6   **keep'st ... conveniency**: deny me any real opportunity

176   **advantage**: increase

178   **put up in peace**: patiently put up with

181–2   **words ... together**: deeds do not match your words

184–5   **wasted ... means**: spent all I had

186   **votarist**: nun

188   **expectations**: promises
      comforts ... respect: encouragement that she will immediately consider me (as a suitor)

189   **acquaintance**: meeting with her

190   **go to**: all right / if you insist

THINK ABOUT for GCSE

Themes and issues

• **Truth and deception**: In what ways has Iago been deceiving and cheating Roderigo? Think about what he has managed to get out of him and how.

Performance and staging

• If you were the director, how would you want Roderigo to behave after his entrance here (lines 171 to 189)?

Iago	I pray you be content. 'Tis but his humour.
	The business of the state does him offence,
	And he does chide with you.

165

Desdemona	If 'twere no other!

Iago	It is but so, I warrant.

Trumpet-calls are heard.

– Hark how these instruments summon you to supper!
The messengers of Venice stay the meat.
Go in, and weep not. All things shall be well.

170

Exit Desdemona, *with* Emilia.

Enter Roderigo.

How now, Roderigo?

Roderigo	I do not find that thou deal'st justly with me.

Iago	What in the contrary?

Roderigo	Every day thou daff'st me with some device, Iago, and
	rather, as it seems to me now, keep'st from me all
	conveniency than suppliest me with the least advantage
	of hope. I will indeed no longer endure it – nor am I
	yet persuaded to put up in peace what already I have
	foolishly suffered.

175

Iago	Will you hear me, Roderigo?

180

Roderigo	Faith, I have heard too much – for your words and
	performances are no kin together.

Iago	You charge me most unjustly.

Roderigo	With naught but truth. I have wasted myself out of my
	means. The jewels you have had from me to deliver to
	Desdemona would half have corrupted a votarist. You
	have told me she hath received them, and returned
	me expectations and comforts of sudden respect and
	acquaintance – but I find none.

185

Iago	Well, go to – very well.

190

Roderigo threatens to go to Desdemona and ask for the return of the jewels he has given her. Iago tells him that Desdemona and Othello will soon be leaving Cyprus and Cassio made governor, unless their departure can be delayed.

THINK ABOUT *for* **GCSE**

Structure and form

- In what ways are Roderigo's threats (lines 195 to 201) important to the development of the plot at this point?

Characterisation

- How does Iago adapt his responses to Roderigo when he hears what he has to say? Compare Iago's opening responses (lines 194 and 199) with his reaction at lines 202 to 206. What does Roderigo say which forces Iago to change his approach?

---

192   **scurvy**: bad behaviour
193   **fopped**: cheated / duped

197   **suit**: request
      solicitation: wooing
198   **seek satisfaction**: i.e. demand his money and jewels back
200   **protest intendment**: declare the intention

202   **mettle**: spirit / courage

204–5 **taken ... exception**: objected very fairly to my behaviour
205   **protest**: assure you
206   **directly**: straightforwardly
207   **It ... appeared**: That's not the way it has looked to me
209   **wit**: intelligence

214   **devise engines for**: invent plots against
215   **compass**: practical possibility

220   **Mauritania**: the land of the Moors in North Africa
221   **abode be lingered**: stay be lengthened
222   **determinate**: decisive

RODERIGO	Very well? Go to? I cannot go to, man, nor 'tis *not* very well. By this hand, I say 'tis very scurvy, and begin to find myself fopped in it.
IAGO	Very well.
RODERIGO	I tell you 'tis not very well! I will make myself known to 195 Desdemona. If she will return me my jewels, I will give over my suit and repent my unlawful solicitation. If not, assure yourself I will seek satisfaction of you.
IAGO	You have said now?
RODERIGO	Ay – and said nothing but what I protest intendment of 200 doing.
IAGO	Why, now I see there's mettle in thee, and even from this instant do build on thee a better opinion than ever before. Give me thy hand, Roderigo. Thou hast taken against me a most just exception – but yet I protest I 205 have dealt most directly in thy affair.
RODERIGO	It hath not appeared.
IAGO	I grant indeed it hath not appeared, and your suspicion is not without wit and judgement. But Roderigo, if thou hast that in thee indeed which I have greater reason to 210 believe now than ever – I mean purpose, courage, and valour – this night show it! If thou the next night following enjoy not Desdemona, take me from this world with treachery and devise engines for my life.
RODERIGO	Well, what is it? Is it within reason and compass? 215
IAGO	Sir, there is especial commission come from Venice to depute Cassio in Othello's place.
RODERIGO	Is that true? Why, then Othello and Desdemona return again to Venice.
IAGO	O, no: he goes into Mauritania and takes away with him 220 the fair Desdemona, unless his abode be lingered here by some accident – wherein none can be so determinate as the removing of Cassio.
RODERIGO	How do you mean, 'removing' of him?

Iago starts to persuade Roderigo to kill Cassio that night.

228 **profit**: good turn
229 **harlotry**: whore
thither: there
230 **fortune**: i.e. being made governor when Othello leaves
231 **watch ... thence**: watch out for him leaving
fashion ... out: arrange to take place
232–3 **take ... pleasure**: attack him whenever it suits you
233 **second**: back up
234 **amazed**: looking bewildered
237 **high**: fully
237–8 **grows to waste**: is passing
238 **About it**: Let's get going

THINK ABOUT *for* GCSE

Language
- What euphemisms does Iago at first employ when referring to the murder of Cassio (lines 220 to 223)? What possibilities are there for comedy in Roderigo's question and Iago's response (lines 224 to 226)?

Characterisation
- What does this scene reveal about Roderigo?
- How much of the plan Iago outlines (lines 228 to 238) do you think he has worked out beforehand, and how much do you think he has thought up while talking to Roderigo?

| IAGO | Why, by making him uncapable of Othello's place – knocking out his brains. | 225 |

| RODERIGO | And that you would have me to do? | |

| IAGO | Ay, if you dare do yourself a profit and a right. He sups tonight with a harlotry, and thither will I go to him. He knows not yet of his honourable fortune. If you will watch his going thence, which I will fashion to fall out between twelve and one, you may take him at your pleasure. I will be near to second your attempt, and he shall fall between us. Come, stand not amazed at it, but go along with me. I will show you such a necessity in his death that you shall think yourself bound to put it on him. It is now high supper-time, and the night grows to waste. About it! | 230

235 |

| RODERIGO | I will hear further reason for this. | |

| IAGO | And you shall be satisfied. | 240 |

Exeunt.

In this scene ...

- As she prepares for bed, Desdemona sings a sad love song.
- Desdemona finds it hard to believe that there are women who are unfaithful to their husbands. Emilia expresses the view that if women behave badly, they are simply copying their husbands.

Othello tells Desdemona to go to bed and to dismiss Emilia for the night.

1   **beseech**: beg

7   **on the instant**: straight away
8   **forthwith**: immediately

11   **incontinent**: at once

15   **nightly wearing**: nightclothes

17   **would**: wish

18   **So would not I**: I don't
     doth so approve: thinks so well of
19   **stubbornness**: roughness
     checks: reprimands

22   **All's one**: 1 It doesn't matter; 2 All right
23   **shroud**: wrap (for burial)

THINK ABOUT for GCSE

Performance and staging

- In a film version of *Othello*, where might Lodovico and Othello be holding their conversation (lines 1 to 5)? And where would the exchange between Desdemona and Emilia take place? How might this differ from the way the opening of this scene might have been staged in Shakespeare's Globe?

Structure and form

- How does the text help to build tension at the beginning of this scene? Look particularly at the repeated ideas in lines 7 to 16.

The private rooms of the fortress.

Enter OTHELLO, LODOVICO, DESDEMONA, EMILIA *and attendants.*

LODOVICO	I do beseech you, sir, trouble yourself no further.
OTHELLO	O, pardon me – 'twill do me good to walk.
LODOVICO	Madam, good night. I humbly thank your ladyship.
DESDEMONA	Your honour is most welcome.
OTHELLO	Will you walk, sir? O, Desdemona –

DESDEMONA   My lord?

OTHELLO   Get you to bed on the instant – I will be returned
forthwith. Dismiss your attendant there. Look it be done.

DESDEMONA   I will, my lord.

Exit OTHELLO, *with* LODOVICO *and attendants.*

EMILIA   How goes it now? He looks gentler than he did.

DESDEMONA   He says he will return incontinent.
He hath commanded me to go to bed,
And bade me to dismiss you.

EMILIA   Dismiss me?

DESDEMONA   It was his bidding – therefore, good Emilia,
Give me my nightly wearing, and adieu.
We must not now displease him.

EMILIA   I would you had never seen him!

DESDEMONA   So would not I. My love doth so approve him
That even his stubbornness, his checks, his frowns –
Prithee unpin me – have grace and favour.

EMILIA   I have laid those sheets you bade me on the bed.

DESDEMONA   All's one. Good faith, how foolish are our minds!
If I do die before thee, prithee shroud me
In one of those same sheets.

5

10

15

20

Desdemona prepares for bed. Upset by Othello's behaviour, she sings a song about a girl whose lover left her.

24 You talk: That's just silly talk

27 forsake: desert
Willow: A tree associated with deserted lovers.
30–1 I have … But: It's all I can do not

32 dispatch: hurry up

33 nightgown: dressing gown

35 proper: good-looking

39 nether: lower

THINK ABOUT for GCSE

Performance and staging
• Which short instructions from Desdemona between lines 20 and 50 act as stage directions to tell the actors what they should be doing in this part of the scene?

Structure and form
• How does Desdemona's song help to set the mood of this scene? How does it create the impression that something bad is about to happen?

47 Lay by these: Put these away

50 hie thee: hurry
anon: very soon

EMILIA	Come, come! You talk.

DESDEMONA	My mother had a maid called Barbary.	25
	She was in love; and he she loved proved mad	
	And did forsake her. She had a song of 'Willow' –	
	An old thing 'twas, but it expressed her fortune,	
	And she died singing it. That song tonight	
	Will not go from my mind. I have much to do	30
	But to go hang my head all at one side	
	And sing it like poor Barbary. – Prithee, dispatch.	

EMILIA	Shall I go fetch your nightgown?

DESDEMONA	No, unpin me here.	
	This Lodovico is a proper man.	35

EMILIA	A very handsome man.

DESDEMONA	He speaks well.

EMILIA	I know a lady in Venice would have walked barefoot
	to Palestine for a touch of his nether lip.

DESDEMONA	(*Singing*)	
	'*The poor soul sat singing by a sycamore tree,*	40
	Sing all a green willow –	
	Her hand on her bosom, her head on her knee,	
	Sing willow, willow, willow.	
	The fresh streams ran by her and murmured her moans,	
	Sing willow, willow, willow –	45
	Her salt tears fell from her, and softened the stones –	
	Sing willow, –'	
	Lay by these. (***Giving some of her clothes to*** EMILIA)	
	'*– willow, willow.*' –	
	Prithee hie thee: he'll come anon.	50
	'*Sing all a green willow must be my garland.*	
	Let nobody blame him; his scorn I approve' –	
	Nay, that's not next. Hark! Who is't that knocks?	

EMILIA	It is the wind.

Desdemona and Emilia
talk about women who are
unfaithful to their husbands.

57   **couch**: go to bed

59   **Doth that bode**: Is that a sign of

61   **in conscience**: really
62   **abuse**: deceive
63   **In … kind**: so obscenely

THINK ABOUT *for* GCSE

Characterisation
* When Emilia says 'by this heavenly light' (line 66) she means 'by the light of the moon'. What does her joke (line 67) tell us about the kind of person she is?

Themes and issues
* **Gender**: What contrasts are drawn in this scene between the attitudes of Emilia and Desdemona to men and marriage? Look, for example, at lines 68 to 83.

69   **price**: prize

70   **troth**: truth

72   **joint-ring**: cheap ring
73   **lawn**: fine white linen
74   **petty exhibition**: small gift or allowance

76–7   **venture purgatory**: risk not going
        straight to heaven

78   **Beshrew**: Curse

DESDEMONA	(*Singing*)
	'*I called my love false love, but what said he then?* **55**
	Sing willow, willow, willow –
	If I court more women, you'll couch with more men.'
	– So, get thee gone. Good night. Mine eyes do itch.
	Doth that bode weeping?
EMILIA	'Tis neither here nor there.
DESDEMONA	I have heard it said so. O, these men, these men! **60**
	Dost thou in conscience think – tell me, Emilia –
	That there be women do abuse their husbands
	In such gross kind?
EMILIA	There be some such, no question.
DESDEMONA	Wouldst thou do such a deed for all the world?
EMILIA	Why, would not you?
DESDEMONA	No, by this heavenly light! **65**
EMILIA	Nor I neither, by this heavenly light –
	I might do it as well i' the dark.
DESDEMONA	Wouldst thou do such a deed for all the world?
EMILIA	The world's a huge thing: it is a great price for a small vice.
DESDEMONA	In troth, I think thou wouldst not. **70**
EMILIA	In troth, I think I should – and undo it when I had done it. Marry, I would not do such a thing for a joint-ring, nor for measures of lawn, nor for gowns, petticoats, nor caps – nor any petty exhibition. But for all the whole world? Why, who would not make her husband a **75** cuckold to make him a monarch? I should venture purgatory for it.
DESDEMONA	Beshrew me if I would do such a wrong for the whole world.
EMILIA	Why, the wrong is but a wrong i' the world – and having **80** the world for your labour, 'tis a wrong in your own world, and you might quickly make it right.
DESDEMONA	I do not think there is any such woman.

Emilia claims that if women behave badly towards their husbands, they are just copying what men do to their wives.

THINK ABOUT *for* **GCSE**

Language
- Emilia's speech in lines 84 to 103 contains several expressions that have an additional sexual meaning. What effect does this speech have at this point in the play?

Themes and issues
- What is the main point Emilia is making here? How does she build up her argument, and what does it contribute to the theme of **gender**?

84 **to the vantage**: in addition
85 **Store**: populate

87 **slack their duties**: 1 neglect their duties; 2 stop having sex with their wives
88 **pour ... laps**: 1 give jewels that should be ours to other women; 2 have sex with other women
89 **peevish**: bad-tempered
90 **Throwing ... upon us**: limiting our freedom
91 **scant ... having**: give us less money
   in despite: to spite us
92 **galls**: 1 tempers; 2 resentment
97 **change**: exchange
   sport: sexual pleasure
98 **affection**: passion
99 **frailty ... errs**: weakness that causes men to behave in this way
103 **The ills ... so**: if we behave badly, it's because we have learned from men
104 **uses**: good habits
105 **Not ... mend**: not to copy bad behaviour, but to learn from it and do better

EMILIA	Yes, a dozen – and as many to the vantage as would
	Store the world they played for. 85
	But I do think it is their husbands' faults
	If wives do fall. Say that they slack their duties
	And pour our treasures into foreign laps,
	Or else break out in peevish jealousies,
	Throwing restraint upon us – or say they strike us, 90
	Or scant our former having in despite –
	Why, we have galls – and though we have some grace,
	Yet have we some revenge. Let husbands know
	Their wives have sense like them. They see, and smell,
	And have their palates both for sweet and sour, 95
	As husbands have. What is it that they do
	When they change us for others? Is it sport?
	I think it is. And doth affection breed it?
	I think it doth. Is't frailty that thus errs?
	It is so too. And have not we affections, 100
	Desires for sport – and frailty – as men have?
	Then let them use us well: else let them know,
	The ills we do, their ills instruct us so.
DESDEMONA	Good night, good night. God me such uses send,
	Not to pick bad from bad, but by bad mend! 105

Exeunt.

In this scene ...

- Roderigo attacks Cassio under cover of darkness as he leaves Bianca's house. In the fight that follows, both men are wounded.
- Iago slyly stabs Roderigo and then, in front of Lodovico and Gratiano, accuses Bianca of being involved in the attack on Cassio.

Roderigo prepares to attack Cassio. Iago intends that both Roderigo and Cassio will die.

THINK ABOUT for **GCSE**

Characterisation

- How much sympathy do you have for Roderigo at the beginning of this scene? How does Roderigo's aside (lines 8 to 10) affect your feelings about him?

- What reasons does Iago give us for wanting the deaths of both Cassio and Roderigo? In particular what does Iago mean when he says of Cassio 'He hath a daily beauty in his life / That makes me ugly' in lines 19 to 20?

1 **bulk**: part of a building that juts out
straight: straight away
2 **Wear ... bare**: Have your sword drawn
put it home: thrust your sword into him
4 **mars**: ruins

6 **miscarry in't**: make a mistake

8 **devotion to**: enthusiasm for

11 **quat**: boil / pimple
to the sense: raw

14 **Every ... gain**: I win either way
Live Roderigo: If Roderigo survives
15 **calls ... large**: will make me give back a large amount
16 **bobbed**: swindled

21 **unfold**: expose

23 **gait**: footstep

24 **had**: would have
25 **But**: were it not
26 **make ... thine**: put yours to the test

Cyprus: a street below the fortress, at night.

Enter IAGO *and* RODERIGO.

IAGO	Here, stand behind this bulk: straight will he come.
	Wear thy good rapier bare, and put it home.
	Quick, quick! Fear nothing – I'll be at thy elbow.
	It makes us, or it mars us, think on that,
	And fix most firm thy resolution.

RODERIGO   Be near at hand: I may miscarry in't.

IAGO   Here, at thy hand. Be bold, and take thy stand.

He moves aside.

RODERIGO   I have no great devotion to the deed,
And yet he hath given me satisfying reasons.
'Tis but a man gone. Forth my sword! He dies!

IAGO   (*Aside*) I have rubbed this young quat almost to the
sense,
And he grows angry. Now, whether he kill Cassio,
Or Cassio him, or each do kill the other,
Every way makes my gain. Live Roderigo,
He calls me to a restitution large
Of gold and jewels that I bobbed from him
As gifts to Desdemona.
It must not be. If Cassio do remain,
He hath a daily beauty in his life
That makes me ugly. And besides, the Moor
May unfold me to him: there stand I in much peril.
No, he must die. Be 't so! (*Drawing his own sword*)
– I hear him coming.

Enter CASSIO.

RODERIGO   I know his gait. 'Tis he. – Villain, thou diest!

He attacks CASSIO.

CASSIO   That thrust had been mine enemy indeed
But that my coat is better than thou know'st.
I will make proof of thine!

5

10

15

20

25

Roderigo and Cassio fight. Iago wounds Cassio from behind. Hearing his cries, Othello thinks that Cassio has been killed. Lodovico and Gratiano arrive on the scene.

27 **maimed**: disabled

31 **brave**: excellent

33 **Minion**: Darling
34 **unblessed**: damned
   hies: approaches swiftly
   Strumpet: Whore
35 **Forth**: From out
   blotted: erased

37 **watch**: watchmen
   passage: passers-by
38 **'Tis some mischance**: Something bad has happened
   direful: dreadful / distressed

42 **heavy**: dark
43 **counterfeits**: thieves pretending to be injured
44 **come in to the cry**: 1 go towards the sound of the cries; 2 get involved

47 **Here's one**: Someone's coming

THINK ABOUT *for* GCSE

Performance and staging

- The stage direction after line 26, which has Iago wounding Cassio and running away, was not written by Shakespeare, and it is only one explanation of what happens. How else could Cassio come to be wounded? If you were the director, how would you stage this?

- What makes Othello's appearance in lines 28 to 36 difficult to stage? Think about what Othello should (and shouldn't) be able to see and hear.

He draws his sword and fights with RODERIGO, *who is wounded.*
IAGO *darts out, wounds* CASSIO *in the leg from behind, and runs*
away.

RODERIGO	O, I am slain!
CASSIO	I am maimed for ever. Help, ho! Murder! Murder!

Enter OTHELLO, *at a distance.*

OTHELLO	(*Aside*) The voice of Cassio! Iago keeps his word.	
RODERIGO	O villain that I am!	
OTHELLO	(*Aside*) It is even so!	
CASSIO	O help, ho! Light! A surgeon!	30
OTHELLO	(*Aside*) 'Tis he. O brave Iago, honest and just,	
	That hast such noble sense of thy friend's wrong!	
	Thou teachest me. Minion, your dear lies dead –	
	And your unblessed fate hies. Strumpet, I come!	
	Forth of my heart those charms, thine eyes, are blotted:	35
	Thy bed, lust-stained, shall with lust's blood be spotted!	

Exit.

Enter LODOVICO *and* GRATIANO.

CASSIO	What, ho? No watch? No passage? Murder! Murder!	
GRATIANO	'Tis some mischance! – the cry is very direful.	
CASSIO	O, help!	
LODOVICO	Hark!	40
RODERIGO	O wretched villain!	
LODOVICO	Two or three groan! It is a heavy night.	
	These may be counterfeits. Let's think't unsafe	
	To come in to the cry without more help.	
RODERIGO	Nobody come? Then shall I bleed to death!	45
LODOVICO	Hark!	

Re-enter IAGO (*as if from bed*) *with a lantern.*

GRATIANO	Here's one comes in his shirt, with light and weapons.

Cassio identifies Roderigo as his attacker. Iago stabs Roderigo.

51 ancient: standard-bearer

53 What: Who

54 spoiled: finished (i.e. fatally wounded)
undone: destroyed

THINK ABOUT *for* GCSE

Context
- Most of Shakespeare's plays, including *Othello*, were first performed in daylight. How does the dialogue in this scene tell us that it is night and that the characters cannot clearly see what is going on?

Language
- What is the effect of the dramatic irony at line 52?

66 As … us: Judge us by our actions

69 I cry you mercy: I beg your pardon

IAGO	Who's there? Whose noise is this that cries on murder?
LODOVICO	We do not know.
IAGO	Do not you hear a cry?
CASSIO	Here, here! For heaven's sake, help me!
IAGO	What's the matter? 50
GRATIANO	This is Othello's ancient, as I take it.
LODOVICO	The same indeed, a very valiant fellow.
IAGO	What are you here that cry so grievously?
CASSIO	Iago? – O, I am spoiled – undone by villains! Give me some help. 55
IAGO	O me, lieutenant! What villains have done this?
CASSIO	I think that one of them is hereabout And cannot make away.
IAGO	O treacherous villains! (*To* LODOVICO *and* GRATIANO) What are you there? Come in, and give some help.
RODERIGO	O, help me there! 60
CASSIO	That's one of them.
IAGO	O murderous slave! O villain!

He stabs RODERIGO.

RODERIGO	O damned Iago! – O inhuman dog!

He faints.

IAGO	Kill men i' the dark? – Where be these bloody thieves? – How silent is this town! – Ho! Murder! Murder! – (*To* LODOVICO *and* GRATIANO) What may you be? Are you of good or evil? 65
LODOVICO	As you shall prove us, praise us.
IAGO	Signior Lodovico?
LODOVICO	He, sir.
IAGO	I cry you mercy. Here's Cassio hurt by villains.

When Bianca enters, Iago suggests that she has been involved in the attack upon Cassio.

72 Marry: By the Virgin Mary

78 notable: notorious
79 mangled: wounded

THINK ABOUT for GCSE

Characterisation

• Do Iago's instructions to Roderigo in Act 4 Scene 2, lines 228 to 238 suggest that he has planned to accuse Bianca of involvement in the attack on Cassio? Or is this an example of his ability to take advantage of fortunate circumstances?

• Iago cannot have known that men as high-ranking as Lodovico and Gratiano would arrive on the scene. How does he quickly exploit their presence when Bianca enters?

85 trash: i.e. Bianca
86 a party: involved

93 cry: ask

95 neglected: ignored / failed to recognise

GRATIANO	Cassio?	70
IAGO	How is it, brother?	
CASSIO	My leg is cut in two.	
IAGO	Marry, heaven forbid! Light, gentlemen. – I'll bind it with my shirt.	

Enter BIANCA.

BIANCA	What is the matter, ho? Who is't that cried?	
IAGO	Who is't that cried?	75
BIANCA	O my dear Cassio! My sweet Cassio! O Cassio, Cassio, Cassio!	
IAGO	O notable strumpet! – Cassio, may you suspect Who they should be that have thus mangled you?	
CASSIO	No.	80
GRATIANO	I am sorry to find you thus. I have been to seek you.	
IAGO	Lend me a garter – so – O for a chair To bear him easily hence!	
BIANCA	Alas, he faints! O Cassio, Cassio, Cassio!	
IAGO	Gentlemen all, I do suspect this trash To be a party in this injury. – Patience awhile, good Cassio. – Come, come. Lend me a light. – Know we this face or no? Alas! – my friend and my dear countryman! Roderigo? No – yes, sure – O heaven, Roderigo!	85 90
GRATIANO	What, of Venice?	
IAGO	Even he, sir. Did you know him?	
GRATIANO	Know him? Ay.	
IAGO	Signior Gratiano? I cry your gentle pardon. These bloody accidents must excuse my manners That so neglected you.	
GRATIANO	I am glad to see you.	95
IAGO	How do you, Cassio? – O, a chair, a chair!	

As Cassio is carried off, Iago continues to accuse Bianca, who admits that Cassio has been at her house that evening.

98 **well said**: well done

100 **For**: As for

101 **Save ... labour**: stop trying to help

102 **malice**: ill feeling

104 **bear ... air**: carry him indoors

106 **gastness of**: frightened look in

109 **speak**: reveal itself
110 **Though ... use**: i.e. without words

117 **know of**: find out from

119 **therefore shake not**: am not trembling through guilt

120 **charge**: order
121 **fie upon thee**: shame on you

THINK ABOUT *for* **GCSE**

Performance and staging
• What do Iago's words to Bianca tell us about the way she might act here (lines 105 to 110)?

Themes and issues
• **Gender**: How does Iago try to make Bianca the chief suspect in the attack on Cassio? Look at the names he calls her (lines 78 and 85) and the methods he uses in lines 105 to 110 and 116 to 120.

GRATIANO	Roderigo?
IAGO	He, – he 'tis he.

Attendants enter, bringing a chair.

– O, that's well said – the chair! –
Some good man bear him carefully from hence.
I'll fetch the general's surgeon. (*To* BIANCA) For you,
   mistress –   **100**
Save you your labour. (*To* CASSIO) He that lies slain
   here, Cassio,
Was my dear friend. What malice was between you?

CASSIO	None in the world – nor do I know the man.
IAGO	What, look you pale? – O, bear him out o' the air!

Attendants carry CASSIO *away in the chair: others carry*
                                        RODERIGO.

– Stay you, good gentlemen. – (*To* BIANCA) Look you
   pale, mistress?   **105**
– Do you perceive the gastness of her eye?
(*To* BIANCA) Nay, if you stare we shall hear more anon.
– Behold her well! – I pray you look upon her –
Do you see, gentlemen? Nay, guiltiness will speak,
Though tongues were out of use.   **110**

Enter EMILIA.

EMILIA	Alas, what's the matter? What's the matter, husband?
IAGO	Cassio hath here been set on in the dark By Roderigo, and fellows that are 'scaped. He's almost slain, and Roderigo quite dead.
EMILIA	Alas, good gentleman! Alas, good Cassio! **115**
IAGO	This is the fruits of whoring! – Prithee, Emilia, Go know of Cassio where he supped tonight. (*To* BIANCA) What, do you shake at that?
BIANCA	He supped at my house – but I therefore shake not.
IAGO	O, did he so? I charge you go with me. **120**
EMILIA	Oh fie upon thee, strumpet!

Iago sends Emilia to tell Othello and Desdemona what has happened. For Iago, everything now hangs upon the events of the night to come.

122 honest: virtuous

123 foh: an expression of disgust

124 see … dressed: get Cassio's wounds treated

126 citadel: fortress

128 afore: ahead

129 fordoes me quite: completely ruins me

THINK ABOUT for GCSE

Structure and form
- Iago says, 'This is the night / That either makes me or fordoes me quite' (lines 128 to 129). What has to happen for Iago's plots to succeed? What can go wrong?

Language
- What is the effect of the rhyme in Iago's parting comment?

BIANCA	I am no strumpet, but of life as honest As you that thus abuse me.
EMILIA	As I? – foh! Fie upon thee!
IAGO	Kind gentlemen, let's go see poor Cassio dressed. (*To* BIANCA) Come, mistress, you must tell's another tale. **125** – Emilia, run you to the citadel And tell my lord and lady what hath happed.

Exit EMILIA.

– Will you go on afore?

All except** IAGO **move away.

– This is the night
That either makes me or fordoes me quite.

Exit.

In this scene ...

- Convinced that Desdemona has been unfaithful, Othello kills her.
- Othello tells Emilia that it was Iago who told him that Desdemona was having an affair with Cassio.
- Realising what Iago has done, Emilia reveals that she had given him the handkerchief, and Iago kills her. Iago refuses to explain any of his actions.
- Asking for people to report his deeds fairly, Othello kills himself.

Othello enters Desdemona's bedroom, preparing to kill her. When Desdemona wakes, Othello tells her to say her prayers.

1   **cause**: reason (for killing Desdemona)
2   **chaste**: (sexually) pure

4   **that ... snow**: her skin, which is whiter than snow
5   **monumental alabaster**: white stone used for tombs
7   **light**: lamp
     light: her life
8   **flaming minister**: i.e. the lamp
11 **thou ... nature**: you beautiful creation of nature at its most perfect
12 **Promethean**: In Greek mythology Prometheus gave fire to humans.
13 **relume**: relight
14 **vital**: living

16 **balmy**: perfumed
17 **break her sword**: not to carry out the punishment

20 **So ... fatal**: Nothing as sweet as this kiss was ever so deadly

THINK ABOUT for GCSE

Performance and staging
- If you were the director, how would you stage the opening of this scene in a modern theatre? What are the difficulties involved?

Language
- When Othello was at his most emotional and out of control his language was disconnected and full of crude expressions (for example, Act 4 Scene 1, lines 36 to 44 and 245 to 256). How does his language at the beginning of this scene (lines 1 to 41) suggest to you that he has regained his calmness and control?

Inside the fortress: Desdemona's bedroom.

Enter OTHELLO, *with a light;* DESDEMONA *is sleeping in her bed.*

OTHELLO	It is the cause, it is the cause, my soul.

It is the cause, it is the cause, my soul.
Let me not name it to you, you chaste stars.
It is the cause. – Yet I'll not shed her blood,
Nor scar that whiter skin of hers than snow,
And smooth as monumental alabaster.   5
Yet she must die, else she'll betray more men.
Put out the light, and then put out the light.
If I quench thee, thou flaming minister,
I can again thy former light restore,
Should I repent me. But once put out *thy* light,   10
Thou cunning'st pattern of excelling nature,
I know not where is that Promethean heat
That can thy light relume. When I have plucked the
      rose,
I cannot give it vital growth again –
It needs must wither. I'll smell it on the tree.   15

He kisses her.

O balmy breath – that dost almost persuade
Justice to break her sword! – One more, one more!
Be thus when thou art dead, and I will kill thee
And love thee after. One more, and this the last.
So sweet was ne'er so fatal. I must weep –   20
But they are cruel tears. This sorrow's heavenly:
It strikes where it doth love. She wakes.

DESDEMONA   Who's there? – Othello?

OTHELLO   Ay, Desdemona.

DESDEMONA   Will you come to bed, my lord?

OTHELLO   Have you prayed tonight, Desdemona?

DESDEMONA   Ay, my lord.   25

Othello tells Desdemona that he is going to kill her and accuses her of giving the handkerchief to Cassio.

26 **bethink yourself of**: remember
27 **Unreconciled … grace**: that you have not yet begged God to forgive
28 **Solicit**: pray God for forgiveness **straight**: at once
29 **Alack**: Alas
31 **unpreparèd**: i.e. not ready to go to heaven
32 **forfend**: forbid

37 **fatal**: deadly

43 **nether**: lower
44 **very frame**: whole body
45 **portents**: bad signs
46 **do … me**: are not a sign of what will happen to me **Peace**: Be quiet

THINK ABOUT for GCSE

Themes and issues

• **Race**: In some productions lines 38 and 43, which describe Othello's behaviour, are cut. Why might these descriptions have been important for the audience in Shakespeare's theatre? Why might modern actors prefer to cut them?

Performance and staging

• If you were the director, how would you want Desdemona to act in this scene? Think about her reaction to Othello's accusation about the handkerchief (lines 49 to 50) and when she realises that Othello intends to kill her.

OTHELLO	If you bethink yourself of any crime Unreconciled as yet to heaven and grace, Solicit for it straight.
DESDEMONA	Alack, my lord, what may you mean by that?
OTHELLO	Well, do it, and be brief. I will walk by. 30 I would not kill thy unpreparèd spirit. No – heaven forfend! – I would not kill thy soul.
DESDEMONA	Talk you of killing?
OTHELLO	Ay, I do.
DESDEMONA	Then heaven Have mercy on me!
OTHELLO	Amen, with all my heart!
DESDEMONA	If you say so, I hope you will not kill me. 35
OTHELLO	Humh!
DESDEMONA	And yet I fear you – for you're fatal then When your eyes roll so. Why I should fear I know not, Since guiltiness I know not – but yet I feel I fear.
OTHELLO	Think on thy sins.
DESDEMONA	They are loves I bear to you. 40
OTHELLO	Ay – and for that thou diest.
DESDEMONA	That death's unnatural that kills for loving. Alas, why gnaw you so your nether lip? Some bloody passion shakes your very frame. These are portents – but yet I hope, I hope, 45 They do not point on me.
OTHELLO	Peace, and be still!
DESDEMONA	I will so. What's the matter?
OTHELLO	That handkerchief which I so loved and gave thee, Thou gav'st to Cassio.
DESDEMONA	No, by my life and soul! Send for the man and ask him.

Desdemona denies having had an affair with Cassio, but Othello tells her that Cassio has admitted it and is now dead.

51 **perjury**: lying while under oath

52 **presently**: immediately
53 **freely**: without holding anything back
54 **article**: point
55 **choke ... conception**: wipe away the powerful belief
56 **groan withal**: am tormented by

59 **Offend**: sin against
60 **But**: except
60–1 **general ... love**: permission from God that we all have to love our fellow creatures
63 **stone**: turn to stone

THINK ABOUT for GCSE

Relationships
• Look at lines 32, 34, 50 to 51 and 56 to 57. What do they suggest about Othello's attitude to Desdemona here?

Characterisation
• Which lines show that Othello has been thinking of what he has to do not as a murder, but as a necessary sacrifice? Look at what he says on this page, and also earlier, at line 6 and lines 21 to 22.

67 **hither**: here

70 **used thee**: had sex with you

Unlawfully: i.e. Outside marriage

73 **ta'en order for**: dealt with

75 **Had ... lives**: Even if he had as many lives as hairs on his head
76 **stomach**: 1 appetite; 2 capacity

OTHELLO	Sweet soul, take heed – **50**
	Take heed of perjury: thou art on thy death-bed.
DESDEMONA	Ay, but not yet to die.
OTHELLO	Yes – presently.
	Therefore confess thee freely of thy sin –
	For to deny each article with oath
	Cannot remove nor choke the strong conception **55**
	That I do groan withal. Thou art to die.
DESDEMONA	Then Lord have mercy on me!
OTHELLO	I say, amen.
DESDEMONA	And have you mercy too! I never did
	Offend you in my life – never loved Cassio
	But with such general warranty of heaven **60**
	As I might love. I never gave him token.
OTHELLO	By heaven, I saw my handkerchief in's hand!
	O perjured woman! – Thou dost stone my heart,
	And mak'st me call what I intend to do
	A murder, which I thought a sacrifice. **65**
	I saw the handkerchief.
DESDEMONA	He found it then.
	I never gave it him. Send for him hither.
	Let him confess a truth.
OTHELLO	He hath confessed.
DESDEMONA	What, my lord?
OTHELLO	That he hath used thee.
DESDEMONA	How? – Unlawfully? **70**
OTHELLO	Ay.
DESDEMONA	He will not say so.
OTHELLO	No. His mouth is stopped.
	Honest Iago hath ta'en order for it.
DESDEMONA	O, my fear interprets! What, is he dead?
OTHELLO	Had all his hairs been lives, my great revenge **75**
	Had stomach for them all.

Othello smothers Desdemona. Emilia arrives outside the door and calls to him urgently.

78 **strumpet**: whore

79 **banish me**: send me away

82 **strive**: struggle

83 **But ... hour**: Let me live just half an hour more
Being ... pause: Now that I have started, I cannot stop

THINK ABOUT for GCSE

Performance and staging

• The stage direction says that Othello smothers Desdemona (line 85), whereas earlier he has agreed to strangle her (see Act 4 Scene 1, lines 203 to 205). If you were the director, how would you want this to be performed? For example, bearing in mind what you know about Othello, should he use a pillow or kill her with his bare hands? What does Othello do as he says 'So, so' (line 90)?

Language

• What does the language of lines 92 to 99 suggest about Othello's emotional state?

92 **By and by**: I'll be with you in a minute
93 **like**: likely that
94 **noise was high**: commotion was loud

99 **insupportable**: unbearable

DESDEMONA	Alas, he is betrayed, and I undone!
OTHELLO	Out, strumpet! – Weep'st thou for him to my face?
DESDEMONA	O banish me, my lord, but kill me not!
OTHELLO	Down, strumpet! 80
DESDEMONA	Kill me tomorrow! Let me live tonight!
OTHELLO	Nay, if you strive –
DESDEMONA	But half an hour!
OTHELLO	Being done, there is no pause.
DESDEMONA	But while I say one prayer!
OTHELLO	It is too late.
DESDEMONA	O, Lord, Lord, Lord! 85

He smothers her.

EMILIA *comes to the door.*

EMILIA	(*Calling*) My lord, my lord! What, ho, my lord, my lord!
OTHELLO	What noise is this? Not dead? – Not yet quite dead? I that am cruel am yet merciful – I would not have thee linger in thy pain. – So, so.
EMILIA	(*Calling*) What, ho! My lord, my lord!
OTHELLO	Who's there? 90
EMILIA	(*Calling*) O, good my lord, I would speak a word with you.
OTHELLO	Yes – 'tis Emilia. – By and by. – She's dead. – 'Tis like she comes to speak of Cassio's death. The noise was high. – Ha! No more moving? Still as the grave. – Shall she come in? Were't good? – 95 I think she stirs again. No. – What's best to do? If she come in, she'll sure speak to my wife. My wife! My wife! What wife? – I have no wife. O, insupportable! O heavy hour!

As Emilia is telling Othello about the attack on Cassio, Desdemona stirs.

101 **affrighted globe**: frightened earth

102 **yawn**: split open (in an earthquake)
alteration: change in nature
(i.e. because Desdemona is dead)
beseech: beg

105 **Soft**: Wait

110 **error**: straying off its normal course

111 **was wont**: used to do / usually does

THINK ABOUT *for* GCSE

Performance and staging
• How should Othello behave as he lets Emilia in (lines 104 to 106)?

Characterisation
• What do Othello's references to astronomical events and their supposed effects (lines 100 to 102, and 110 to 112) suggest about him at this point?

120 **Out and alas**: an expression of grief

Methinks it should be now a huge eclipse   100
Of sun and moon, and that th' affrighted globe
Should yawn at alteration.

EMILIA   (*Calling again*) I do beseech you
That I may speak with you, O good my lord!

OTHELLO   I had forgot thee. – O, come in Emilia.
Soft, by and by. – Let me the curtains draw. –   105

He draws the bed-curtains round it, then goes to the door.

Where art thou?

Enter EMILIA.

What's the matter with thee now?

EMILIA   O my good lord, yonder's foul murders done!

OTHELLO   What? Now?

EMILIA   But now, my lord.

OTHELLO   It is the very error of the moon: 110
She comes more near earth than she was wont
And makes men mad.

EMILIA   Cassio, my lord, hath killed a young Venetian
Called Roderigo.

OTHELLO   Roderigo killed?
And Cassio killed?

EMILIA   No, Cassio is not killed.   115

OTHELLO   Not Cassio killed! – Then murder's out of tune,
And sweet revenge grows harsh.

DESDEMONA   O – falsely, falsely murdered!

EMILIA   O Lord! What cry is that?

OTHELLO   That? What?

EMILIA   Out and alas! – That was my lady's voice!   120

She rushes to the bed and draws back its curtains.

Help, help, ho! Help! – O lady, speak again!
Sweet Desdemona! O sweet mistress, speak!

With her dying breath Desdemona claims that she killed herself. But Othello admits that he has committed the murder, adding that Iago had told him that Desdemona was unfaithful.

126 Commend me to: Give my love to

127 should she be: could she have been

130 like a liar: like the liar that she is

133 folly: sexual immorality

134 belie: slander

THINK ABOUT
for **GCSE**

Characterisation
- Why does Desdemona claim that she has killed herself (lines 125 to 126)? How does this affect your impression of her?

Language
- How does Emilia's language here contrast Desdemona's goodness with Othello's evil, as she sees it?

Themes and issues
- **Race**: Are Emilia's accusations (lines 132 and 134) racist? What do they reveal about her?

137 top: have sex with
    else: if you think it's not true
139 But: except
140 extremity: final punishment

141 false: unfaithful
    wedlock: marriage

144 Of ... chrysolite: out of one pure, perfect golden-green precious stone

DESDEMONA	A guiltless death I die.
EMILIA	O, who hath done this deed?
DESDEMONA	Nobody – I myself. Farewell. 125 Commend me to my kind lord. O, farewell!

She dies.

OTHELLO	Why, how should she be murdered?
EMILIA	Alas, who knows?
OTHELLO	You heard her say herself it was not I.
EMILIA	She said so. I must needs report the truth.
OTHELLO	She's like a liar gone to burning hell! 130 'Twas I that killed her.
EMILIA	O, the more angel she, And you the blacker devil!
OTHELLO	She turned to folly, and she was a whore.
EMILIA	Thou dost belie her, and thou art a devil!
OTHELLO	She was false as water.
EMILIA	Thou art rash as fire to say 135 That she was false. O, she was heavenly true!
OTHELLO	Cassio did top her! – Ask thy husband else. O, I were damned beneath all depth in hell But that I did proceed upon just grounds To this extremity. Thy husband knew it all. 140
EMILIA	My husband?
OTHELLO	Thy husband.
EMILIA	That she was false to wedlock?
OTHELLO	Ay, with Cassio. – Had she been true, If heaven would make me such another world Of one entire and perfect chrysolite, I'd not have sold her for it.
EMILIA	My husband? 145

Determined to expose Othello
as a murderer, Emilia calls for
help. Iago enters with Montano
and Gratiano.

149 **iterance**: repetition

150 **made mocks with**: made a mockery of

154 **pernicious**: poisonous
155 **half ... day**: i.e. slowly
156 **fond of**: foolishly in love with
     filthy bargain: i.e. marriage to Othello

160 **Peace ... best**: You had better be quiet

162 **gull**: gullible fool
     dolt: idiot

164 **make thee known**: reveal what you
     have done

169 **lay ... neck**: blame you when they
     have committed murder

THINK ABOUT for GCSE

Characterisation
• How do Emilia's responses
  here help to show the
  struggle she is having
  in coming to terms with
  the truth about Iago's
  involvement in the murder?

Language
• How is the dramatic irony
  underlined in Othello's
  descriptions of Iago (lines
  147 and 153)?

OTHELLO	Ay, 'twas he that told me on her first.
	An honest man he is, and hates the slime
	That sticks on filthy deeds.

| EMILIA | My husband? |

| OTHELLO | What needs this iterance, woman? I say thy husband. |

| EMILIA | O mistress, villainy hath made mocks with love! | **150** |
| | My husband say that she was false! |

OTHELLO	He, woman.
	I say, thy husband. Dost understand the word?
	My friend – thy husband – honest, honest Iago.

EMILIA	If he say so, may his pernicious soul
	Rot half a grain a day! He lies to th' heart!	**155**
	She was too fond of her most filthy bargain.

| OTHELLO | Ha? |

EMILIA	Do thy worst!
	This deed of thine is no more worthy heaven
	Than thou wast worthy her.

| OTHELLO | Peace, you were best. | **160** |

EMILIA	Thou hast not half that power to do me harm
	As I have to be hurt. O gull! O dolt! –
	As ignorant as dirt! Thou hast done a deed –

OTHELLO *moves to draw his sword.*

	I care not for thy sword – I'll make thee known,
	Though I lost twenty lives. Help! Help ho! Help!	**165**
	The Moor hath killed my mistress! Murder! Murder!

Enter MONTANO, GRATIANO, *and* IAGO, *with attendants.*

| MONTANO | What is the matter? How now, general? |

| EMILIA | O, are *you* come, Iago? You have done well, |
| | That men must lay their murders on your neck. |

| GRATIANO | What is the matter? | **170** |

Emilia bitterly accuses Iago
of having told a disgusting lie
about Desdemona which has
led to her murder.

176   **apt**: likely

179   **odious**: hateful

182   **charm your tongue**: be silent

183   **am bound**: have a duty

185   **forfend**: forbid

THINK ABOUT *for* GCSE

Characterisation

* At what point does Emilia
  become certain that Iago is
  guilty of having deceived
  Othello? What does she
  mean by 'I thought so then'
  (line 191)? For one possible
  interpretation, look back at
  Act 4 Scene 2, lines 129 to
  132.

Context

* Shakespeare's audience
  would have known the
  teaching of St Paul in the
  Bible in which he instructs
  wives to be subordinate to
  their husbands. How might
  the audience have reacted
  to Emilia at line 195?

193   **charge**: order

195   **proper**: fitting

199   **lift up eye**: look up to heaven (i.e. to
      pray)

EMILIA	Disprove this villain, if thou be'st a man.
	He says thou told'st him that his wife was false.
	I know thou didst not – thou'rt not such a villain.
	Speak, for my heart is full.
IAGO	I told him what I thought, and told no more 175
	Than what he found himself was apt and true.
EMILIA	But did you ever tell him she was false?
IAGO	I did.
EMILIA	You told a lie, an odious damnèd lie!
	Upon my soul, a lie! – A wicked lie! 180
	She false with Cassio? Did you say with Cassio?
IAGO	With Cassio, mistress. Go to, charm your tongue.
EMILIA	I will *not* charm my tongue. I am bound to speak.
	My mistress here lies murdered in her bed.
ALL	O heavens forfend! 185
EMILIA	– And your reports have set the murder on.
OTHELLO	Nay, stare not, masters. It is true indeed.
GRATIANO	'Tis a strange truth.
MONTANO	O monstrous act!
EMILIA	Villainy, villainy, villainy!
	I think upon't – I think I smell't! – O villainy! 190
	I thought so then. – I'll kill myself for grief. –
	O villainy, villainy!
IAGO	What, are you mad? I charge you get you home.
EMILIA	Good gentlemen, let me have leave to speak.
	'Tis proper I obey him – but not now. 195
	Perchance, Iago, I will ne'er go home.
OTHELLO	O! O! O!

He falls onto the bed.

EMILIA	Nay, lay thee down and roar! –
	For thou hast killed the sweetest innocent
	That e'er did lift up eye.

When Othello mentions the handkerchief, Emilia reveals that she found it and gave it to Iago.

200 **scarce did know**: hardly recognised

204 **Thy ... him**: Your marriage was the death of him
205 **Shore**: cut
twain: two
Did he live: Had he been alive
206 **do a desperate turn**: kill himself
207 **curse ... side**: drive his guardian angel away
208 **reprobation**: damnation (for killing himself)
212 **gratify... works**: reward his love-making
213 **recognizance**: token

THINK ABOUT for GCSE

Structure and form
• What is the effect of letting the audience know that Desdemona's father is dead (lines 203 to 208)?

Characterisation
• What does Emilia's exclamation at line 217 suggest? For example, has she suddenly realised the part she has played in the tragedy? Or is it only here that she fully realises what Iago has done and how he has done it?

218 **Zounds**: God's wounds (a powerful oath)
'Twill out: The truth must come out
219 **liberal as the north**: as freely as the north wind blows

223 **Fie**: You should be ashamed

224 **dull**: stupid

227 **belonged**: was appropriate

OTHELLO	(*Standing again*) O – she was foul!	
	(*To* GRATIANO) I scarce did know you, uncle. There lies	
	your niece,	200
	Whose breath, indeed, these hands have newly stopped.	
	I know this act shows horrible and grim –	

GRATIANO   Poor Desdemona! I am glad thy father's dead.
Thy match was mortal to him, and pure grief
Shore his old thread in twain. Did he live now,   205
This sight would make him do a desperate turn –
Yea, curse his better angel from his side,
And fall to reprobation!

OTHELLO   'Tis pitiful – but yet Iago knows
That she with Cassio hath the act of shame   210
A thousand times committed. Cassio confessed it.
And she did gratify his amorous works
With that recognizance and pledge of love,
Which I first gave her. I saw it in his hand.
It was a handkerchief – an antique token   215
My father gave my mother.

EMILIA   O God! O heavenly God!

IAGO   Zounds, hold your peace!

EMILIA   'Twill out, 'twill out! I – peace?
No, I will speak as liberal as the north.
Let heaven and men and devils, let them all,   220
All, all, cry shame against me, yet I'll speak.

IAGO   Be wise, and get you home!

EMILIA   I will not.

IAGO *threatens* EMILIA *with his sword.*

GRATIANO   Fie! – Your sword upon a woman?

EMILIA   O thou dull Moor, that handkerchief thou speak'st of
I found by fortune, and did give my husband.   225
For often with a solemn earnestness –
More than indeed belonged to such a trifle –
He begged of me to steal it.

IAGO   Villainous whore!

At last realising the truth, Othello tries to kill Iago. In the scuffle, Iago stabs Emilia. As Iago escapes from the room, pursued by Montano and others, Emilia dies. Gratiano remains outside, guarding the door.

232 **coxcomb**: fool

233 **stones**: thunderbolts

238 **notorious**: blatant

240 **without**: from outside

243 **puny**: feeble
     whipster: whippersnapper

245 **bode**: foretell
246 **play the swan**: Swans were believed to sing before their death.

249 **bliss**: i.e. the bliss of heaven

THINK ABOUT for GCSE

Characterisation
- At what point does Othello finally see the truth? How might an audience feel about Othello at this point?
- Why does Iago kill Emilia?
- What is your final impression of Emilia?

EMILIA	She give it Cassio? No, alas – I found it,
	And I did give't my husband.

IAGO	Filth, thou liest!	230

EMILIA	By heaven, I do not – I do not, gentlemen.
	(*To* OTHELLO) O murderous coxcomb! What should
	such a fool
	Do with so good a wife?

OTHELLO	Are there no stones in heaven
	But what serves for the thunder? – Precious villain!

He draws his sword and rushes at IAGO, *but* MONTANO *and others disarm him.*
In the confusion, IAGO *stabs* EMILIA *and escapes.*

GRATIANO	The woman falls! Sure he hath killed his wife.	235

EMILIA	Ay, ay. – O, lay me by my mistress' side.

GRATIANO	He's gone, but his wife's killed.

MONTANO	'Tis a notorious villain! (*To* GRATIANO) Take you this	
	weapon,	
	Which I have here recovered from the Moor.	
	Come – guard the door without. Let him not pass,	240
	But kill him rather. – I'll after that same villain,	
	For 'tis a damnèd slave.	

Exit, with GRATIANO, *and all except* OTHELLO *and* EMILIA.

OTHELLO	I am not valiant neither,
	But every puny whipster gets my sword.
	But why should honour outlive honesty?
	– Let it go all.

EMILIA	What did thy song bode, lady?	245
	Hark, canst thou hear me? I will play the swan,	
	And die in music. – (*She sings*) 'Willow, willow,	
	willow' –	
	Moor, she was chaste. She loved thee, cruel Moor,	
	So come my soul to bliss as I speak true.	
	So speaking as I think, alas, I die.	250

She dies.

Calling Gratiano into the room, and revealing that he is still armed, Othello grieves for his dead wife.

252 **the ice-brook's temper**: hardened in freezing water (i.e. the best steel)

255 **perforce**: inevitably

257 **naked**: unarmed

262 **impediments**: obstacles
263 **your stop**: the obstacle you represent

266 **butt**: goal
267 **sea-mark … sail**: landmark for the end of my final voyage
268 **lost**: pointless
269 **Man but a rush**: Aim only a reed
270 **retires**: retreats

271 **ill-starred wench**: ill-fated woman
272 **smock**: nightdress
compt: Judgement Day

277 **the possession … sight**: owning this vision (of Desdemona's beauty) which should belong to heaven
279 **steep-down gulfs**: steep-sided canyons

THINK ABOUT for GCSE

Characterisation
* How does the opening of Othello's speech (lines 259 to 270) show that he moves quickly from defiance to an acceptance of his fate?

Language
* When Othello cries 'O cursèd, cursèd slave' (line 276) do you think he is referring to Iago or to himself?

OTHELLO	I have another weapon in this chamber –
	It was a sword of Spain, the ice-brook's temper.
	O, here it is. – (*Calling*) Uncle, I must come forth.

GRATIANO	(*From outside the door*) If thou attempt it, it will cost
	thee dear.
	Thou hast no weapon, and perforce must suffer.

255

OTHELLO	Look in upon me then and speak with me,
	Or, naked as I am, I will assault thee.

Re-enter GRATIANO.

GRATIANO	What is the matter?

OTHELLO   Behold, I have a weapon:
A better never did itself sustain
Upon a soldier's thigh. I have seen the day   260
That with this little arm and this good sword
I have made my way through more impediments
Than twenty times your stop. – But O, vain boast!
Who can control his fate? – 'Tis not so now.
Be not afraid, though you do see me weaponed.   265
Here is my journey's end, here is my butt,
And very sea-mark of my utmost sail.
Do you go back dismayed? – 'Tis a lost fear.
Man but a rush against Othello's breast,
And he retires. Where should Othello go?   270

He goes to the bed.

Now – how dost thou look now? O ill-starred wench!
Pale as thy smock! When we shall meet at compt,
This look of thine will hurl my soul from heaven,
And fiends will snatch at it. Cold, cold, my girl? –
Even like thy chastity.   275
O cursèd, cursèd slave! Whip me, ye devils,
From the possession of this heavenly sight!
Blow me about in winds! Roast me in sulphur!
Wash me in steep-down gulfs of liquid fire!
O Desdemona! Dead Desdemona! – Dead!   280
O! O!

239

Iago is brought in as a prisoner, along with the wounded Cassio. Othello asks Cassio's pardon and demands that Iago explain his actions. He refuses.

THINK ABOUT for GCSE

Context

• Iago is not a Venetian name, but Spanish (the equivalent of 'James'). What effect might his name have had upon those members of Shakespeare's audience who knew the story of the eleventh century apostle who fought against the Moors in Spain and was known as 'Santiago Metamoros' ('Saint James the Moor-Killer')?

Themes and issues

• **Reputation and honour**: Which lines show that Othello still believes that he was motivated by a sense of honour rather than hatred or rage?

Performance and staging

• How should Iago speak his final words (lines 302 to 303)? For example, should he appear satisfied with the outcome? Is he gloating? Does he now seem to regret what he has done? Or does he show no emotion at all?

285 **fable**: i.e. it is only a myth that the devil has cloven hooves

289 **in my sense**: the way I feel

291 **in the practice**: through the plots

296 **consent in**: plan together

301 **ensnared**: entrapped

304 **Torments**: Torture
ope: open
305 **dost best**: are wise (to remain silent)

Enter LODOVICO *and* MONTANO, *with* IAGO, *as a prisoner,*
escorted by officers. Attendants bring CASSIO *in a chair.*

LODOVICO	Where is this rash and most unfortunate man?
OTHELLO	That's he that was Othello. Here I am.
LODOVICO	Where is that viper? Bring the villain forth.
OTHELLO	I look down towards his feet – but that's a fable. 285 If that thou be'st a devil, I cannot kill thee.

He wounds IAGO.

LODOVICO	Wrench his sword from him!

OTHELLO *is disarmed.*

IAGO	I bleed, sir, but not killed.
OTHELLO	I am not sorry neither. I'd have thee live – For in my sense, 'tis happiness to die.
LODOVICO	O thou, Othello, that was once so good, 290 Fall'n in the practice of a cursèd slave, What shall be said to thee?
OTHELLO	Why, anything: An honourable murderer, if you will – For naught I did in hate, but all in honour.
LODOVICO	This wretch hath part confessed his villainy. 295 Did you and he consent in Cassio's death?
OTHELLO	Ay.
CASSIO	Dear general, I never gave you cause.
OTHELLO	I do believe it, and I ask your pardon. Will you, I pray, demand that demi-devil 300 Why he hath thus ensnared my soul and body?
IAGO	Demand me nothing. What you know, you know. From this time forth I never will speak word.
LODOVICO	What, not to pray?
GRATIANO	Torments will ope your lips.
OTHELLO	(*To* IAGO) Well, thou dost best. 305

Lodovico produces two letters explaining Iago's plots, which were found on Roderigo's body. Cassio tells Othello that he found the handkerchief in his room after Iago had left it there. Lodovico arrests Othello and makes Cassio governor of Cyprus.

309 imports: is about

312 heathenish: savage
gross: disgusting
313 discontented paper: angry letter

316 But that, belike: except that, most probably
in the nick: i.e. before Roderigo could send it
317 satisfied him: gave him a satisfactory explanation
pernicious caitiff: poisonous slave

322 wrought ... desire: contributed to his plan

THINK ABOUT *for* GCSE

Structure and form

• What part has the handkerchief (lines 318 to 320) played in Othello's downfall?

• What information is provided through Roderigo's letters and his dying words (lines 306 to 328)? How important is this for (a) the audience; and (b) the other characters?

324 upbraids: complains to
325 Brave: provoke
whereon: as a result of which
326 cast: dismissed (as lieutenant)
even but now: only a moment ago

329 forsake: leave

332 cunning cruelty: skilful torture
333 hold him long: keep him alive a long time in great pain
334 rest: remain

LODOVICO	Sir, you shall understand what hath befallen,
	Which, as I think, you know not. Here is a letter
	Found in the pocket of the slain Roderigo,
	And here another. The one of them imports
	The death of Cassio to be undertook	310
	By Roderigo.

OTHELLO   O villain!

CASSIO   Most heathenish and most gross!

LODOVICO   Now here's another discontented paper
           Found in his pocket too; and this, it seems,
           Roderigo meant to have sent this damnèd villain –   315
           But that, belike, Iago, in the nick,
           Came in and satisfied him.

OTHELLO   (*To* IAGO) O thou pernicious caitiff!
           How came you, Cassio, by that handkerchief
           That was my wife's?

CASSIO   I found it in my chamber –
           And he himself confessed but even now   320
           That there he dropped it for a special purpose
           Which wrought to his desire.

OTHELLO   O fool! Fool! Fool!

CASSIO   There is besides in Roderigo's letter,
           How he upbraids Iago that he made him
           Brave me upon the watch – whereon it came   325
           That I was cast. And even but now he spake,
           After long seeming dead – Iago hurt him –
           Iago set him on.

LODOVICO   (*To* OTHELLO) You must forsake this room and go with us.
           Your power and your command is taken off,   330
           And Cassio rules in Cyprus. For this slave,
           If there be any cunning cruelty
           That can torment him much and hold him long,
           It shall be his. You shall close prisoner rest
           Till that the nature of your fault be known   335
           To the Venetian state. – Come, bring away.

Othello asks that people should speak fairly about him. Producing a hidden weapon, he stabs himself and dies next to Desdemona.

337 Soft you: Wait a moment

341 extenuate: tone down

344 wrought: worked upon
345 Perplexed: troubled / bewildered
346–7 Like ... tribe: Indians were believed not to appreciate the value of precious gems.
347 subdued: overcome
348 Albeit: although
the melting mood: tender feelings
350 medicinable gum: sap used as medicine
351 Aleppo: an ancient city in Syria
352 malignant: wicked
353 traduced: insulted
355 smote: struck

356 period: conclusion
marred: ruined

THINK ABOUT for GCSE

Themes and issues
• **Jealousy**: How far would you agree with the view of himself that Othello expresses in lines 343 to 345?

Performance and staging
• In some productions Iago reacts emotionally to Othello's suicide, but in others he seems to be completely unmoved. If you were the director, how would you want Iago to react to Othello's suicide?

360 Spartan dog: Spartan dogs were famed for their ferocity.
361 fell: deadly
363 object: spectacle

364 keep: guard
365 seize upon: confiscate
366 they succeed on you: you inherit them
lord governor: i.e. Cassio (his new position)

OTHELLO	Soft you, a word or two before you go.
	I have done the state some service, and they know it.
	No more of that. I pray you, in your letters,
	When you shall these unlucky deeds relate,	340
	Speak of me as I am. Nothing extenuate,
	Nor set down aught in malice. Then must you speak
	Of one that loved not wisely, but too well;
	Of one not easily jealous, but being wrought,
	Perplexed in the extreme; of one whose hand,	345
	Like the base Indian, threw a pearl away
	Richer than all his tribe; of one whose subdued eyes,
	Albeit unusèd to the melting mood,
	Drops tears as fast as the Arabian trees
	Their medicinable gum. – Set you down this.	350
	And say besides that in Aleppo once,
	Where a malignant and a turbaned Turk
	Beat a Venetian and traduced the state,
	I took by the throat the circumcisèd dog
	And smote him – thus!	355

He stabs himself with a hidden blade.

| LODOVICO | O bloody period! |

| GRATIANO | All that is spoke is marred. |

| OTHELLO | I kissed thee ere I killed thee. No way but this, |
| | Killing myself, to die upon a kiss. |

He falls beside DESDEMONA, *and dies.*

| CASSIO | This did I fear, but thought he had no weapon – |
| | For he was great of heart. |

LODOVICO	(*To* IAGO) O Spartan dog,	360
	More fell than anguish, hunger, or the sea,
	Look on the tragic loading of this bed.
	This is thy work. – The object poisons sight:
	Let it be hid.

The curtains are drawn round the bed.

	Gratiano, keep the house,
	And seize upon the fortunes of the Moor,	365
	For they succeed on you. To you, lord governor,

245

Cassio is given the responsibility for Iago's punishment. Lodovico leaves to break the news in Venice.

367 **censure**: trial and punishment

369 **straight aboard**: immediately board ship

370 **heavy**: sorrowful

THINK ABOUT for GCSE

Structure and form

- In addition to Iago, Cassio, Montano, Gratiano, and Lodovico are all present at the end. What is the status of each of these four characters? Why should Lodovico be given the final speech?

Performance and staging

- Think about the conclusion of *Othello*. If you were directing a film version, what would your final shot be? If you were directing a stage play, what would the final moment look like?

Remains the censure of this hellish villain:
The time, the place, the torture – O, enforce it!
Myself will straight aboard, and to the state
This heavy act with heavy heart relate.   **370**

Exeunt.

Othello is a play about love, hatred and jealousy. It is set mainly on Cyprus during the wars between Venice and the Turks.

AFRICANS IN SHAKESPEARE'S ENGLAND

Shakespeare's audiences would have been quite used to seeing Africans around London. By the time *Othello* was first performed, it had become fashionable among some wealthy Londoners to have African servants (who were often paid employees rather than slaves). Ambassadors from Africa had also visited, causing a real stir with their glamorous dress and different customs.

Elizabethan attitudes to race were not straightforward. There was a thriving European slave trade to the Caribbean in Shakespeare's time, although England was not involved in this until around 50 years later. African servants in London, who were sometimes freed slaves, might have been looked down upon because of their low status, but there is only limited evidence that people looked down upon them simply because they had black skin. It would not have surprised Shakespeare's audiences, therefore, to see a 'Moor' on stage. What might have surprised them, however, was the sight of a black general in charge of a European army. Although this would have been inconceivable in England, it was, in fact, quite usual for foreigners, including Africans, to be in command of Venetian forces. Venice had a population drawn from all over the Mediterranean and beyond and was famed for its tolerance of outsiders. In the play, Othello's position is totally accepted by the Duke, the senators and even by Iago.

The idea of a white woman marrying a black man would have disturbed many people in Shakespeare's audience. At the time, mixed-race marriages were uncommon and frowned upon. Iago makes much of this and it is a major reason behind Brabantio's objection to the marriage between his daughter and Othello. For Brabantio, a European girl falling in love with an African is a sign that the natural order of things has been turned upside down. He believes that only witchcraft could be responsible.

MARRIAGE AND COURTSHIP

In Shakespeare's time it was not always possible for a young woman simply to fall in love and marry the man of her choice. Courtship in powerful or noble families followed certain rules. Any man, no matter how high-ranking, would be expected to ask a young woman's father for permission to woo her. Fathers were powerful figures and their children were expected to do as they were told.

Desdemona's rebellion against the power of her father and her dignified explanation of her love for Othello in front of the Senate show her bravery and independence of spirit, which would have made her an extremely impressive female character in Shakespeare's time.

VILLAINS ON STAGE

Shakespeare's audiences would have been very familiar with the role of 'villain'. Some of the most popular villains appeared in an earlier kind of religious drama called 'Morality Plays'. These plays were extremely popular until as late as 1560 and showed the battle between good and evil for control of a man's soul. On the 'evil' side was a character called the Vice, a representative of the devil. The Vice, a partly comic 'trickster' character, was always conquered in the end, but not before he had had a lot of fun at the expense of the other characters.

The character of Iago partly came out of the Vice tradition. There are many moments of comedy in his rise and fall, especially in his dealings with the rich and stupid Roderigo. Like the Vice, Iago is defeated in the end – though in this case not before he has achieved his aim of destroying Othello and those around him. Where Iago differs from the Vice is in his individuality. The Vice, however brilliantly he is played on stage, is never more than a figure who represents evil, whereas Iago is a frighteningly real and evil human being.

THEATRE AND STAGE

When *Othello* was written (probably in 1604), it would have been intended for performance in the Globe playhouse, the famous theatre in which Shakespeare's acting company, the King's Men, were based. Four or five years later, *Othello* could also have been performed in the company's smaller indoor theatre, the Blackfriars, and we know that there were also performances at court (for King James) and on tour, away from London.

What we know about the staging of plays in the Globe four hundred years ago comes mainly from the evidence of plays, like *Othello*, that we know were performed there. Almost all of the action of this tragedy takes place on the large main-stage platform (roughly thirteen metres wide by nine metres deep). This was clearly big enough for characters to appear on it in separate groups, to 'hide' themselves from others, and to overhear (or not to overhear) what others say, depending on their stage-positions. In Act 2 Scene 1 of *Othello*, while Cassio talks quietly with Desdemona, Iago can offer his vicious commentary on this conversation in an 'aside' to the audience. Later, in Act 4 Scene 1, Iago deceives Othello by stage-managing a scene in which Cassio's talk about Bianca will seem (to Othello) to incriminate Desdemona. 'Withdrawn' to one side of the stage, Othello sees, then comes closer to hear, only what Iago wants him to see and hear. When characters needed to hide behind something, for example when Roderigo is placed 'behind this bulk' to ambush Cassio (Act 5 Scene 1), they may have concealed themselves behind one of the two great pillars that held up the canopy (known as 'the heavens') over the stage. Iago himself, as mastermind of the tragedy's destructive plotting, often seems disturbingly close to audiences, sharing his evil with them in his soliloquies and asides. Sometimes he seems to be almost daring them to 'hiss the villain', for example when he says 'And what's he then that says I play the villain …?' in Act 2 Scene 3.

Only in the first scene, when Brabantio appears 'at a window' when disturbed in the night by Iago and Roderigo, is action specifically called for above the main stage (in the gallery about three metres up on the back-stage wall). *Othello* is otherwise an intimate and claustrophobic tragedy, with no very spectacular staging effects.

The arrival in Cyprus, however, in Act 2 Scene 1, may well have been performed as a 'look-out' scene with players on the stage (the island of Cyprus) watching out for the safe arrival of Othello's ships across the 'sea' of the standing audience in the theatre yard.

ACTION, SETTINGS, PROPS AND DARKNESS

The action of the play in the Globe would have been fast and continuous, with no intervals between acts or scenes. New scenes are often marked simply by the entrance of new characters. When the Duke and Senators of Venice appear in Act 1 Scene 3, they sit at a table that stage-hands would have brought out for them as they enter. Their presence and this change is enough to show that we are no longer out in the dark streets of Venice, but at an indoor council meeting. No scenery or stage lighting, as we think of them, were used. The play's language and activity, along with occasional props (table and chairs, candles or flaming torches, Desdemona's bed near the end of the tragedy), was enough to suggest places or settings to the imagination of its audience.

A play in performance at the reconstruction of Shakespeare's Globe

The outside of Brabantio's house in the opening scene would have been represented only by the rising wall of the dressing-room area behind the stage, with 'window' (stage-balcony) and 'doors' (the two main stage-entrances). This same stage architecture could represent any building, like the fortress of Cyprus, or the back wall of a room for indoor scenes. Between the stage doors would have been a third opening, usually curtained off. This was known as the 'discovery' space, because special items, such as Desdemona's bed for the final 'bedroom' death-scene of *Othello*, could be pushed out from it or revealed ('discovered') inside it. Desdemona's would clearly have been a large four-poster bed, with its own curtains. A luxurious bed, like the wearing of expensive costumes in the play, would have been another signal of the high rank and importance of the main characters, as well as creating and dominating the final tragic 'bedroom' setting.

Roughly half the scenes of *Othello* take place at night, and darknesses are central to the tragedy. Lights are carried or called for in dark streets, both in Venice and Cyprus, not for stage lighting but to show the audience in the open-air afternoon daylight of the Globe that it was watching a 'night-time' scene. Othello himself is of course an exotic 'darkness' (the star tragic actor of Shakespeare's company, Richard Burbage, would probably have played him in dark make-up), and one who tragically 'puts out a light' when he kills Desdemona in Act 5 Scene 2. Other 'Moors' in Elizabethan plays had often been racially stereotyped as 'black' villains. In *Othello*, by contrast, Shakespeare's darkest evil, Iago, is white.

Tears for Desdemona

A letter written in 1610 gives a rare suggestion of the strong effect that the tragic ending of *Othello* had on audiences in Shakespeare's time. A spectator who saw the King's Men perform the play on tour, in an Oxford college hall, reported that the university audience was moved to tears by it. Desdemona, 'killed by her husband' at the end, was especially moving as she died: 'when lying in bed she implored the pity of those watching with her countenance alone.' The female parts in *Othello* (Bianca and Emilia, as well as Desdemona) were played by skilled specialist boy actors in the company. This boy actor had successfully 'become Desdemona', a woman in the eyes of the audience, and his acting, when only his face could be seen, had been powerful enough to make spectators cry.

The destruction of Othello and Desdemona remains one of Shakespeare's most powerful and concentrated tragedies. Staging in Shakespeare's theatre may in some ways seem simple or crude by modern standards, but it was extremely powerful in playing to the imaginations and emotions of its audiences. And those emotions were nearer to the surface of expression than ours often are today. Audiences might shed tears, as well as laugh, together.

The exterior of Shakespeare's Globe

Since its first recorded performance in 1604, *Othello* has been a popular play. There are many different ways of approaching the play in performance and directors ask themselves a number of key questions when they plan to stage it. These include:

- What is Othello's real weakness?
- How should Othello, as a 'Moor', be presented on stage?
- What are Iago's motives?
- How should the women be played to ensure that they are not overshadowed by the powerful figures of Othello and Iago?
- How should he play be staged in order to bring out its key themes?

OTHELLO'S WEAKNESS

As a respected general, Othello is generally portrayed as physically strong and commanding, but what is his key emotional weakness? At the end of the play he describes himself as 'one who loved not wisely but too well', and it is certainly true that Iago uses the power of Othello's love for Desdemona to destroy him. Laurence Fishburne, in particular, in the 1995 **Oliver Parker** film, shows how tormented by jealousy Othello becomes when he is provoked by Iago's lies. However, many actors have felt that Othello's greatest weakness is that he is too trusting, or rather that he trusts the wrong people. One interpretation is that he trusts Iago because he is a soldier, and doesn't trust Desdemona because he has no experience of women. Speaking of his 1952 film, **Orson Welles** described his own Othello as a normally steady man 'destroyed easily because of his simplicity'. Ben Kingsley in the 1985 **RSC** production played Othello as a man apparently strong-willed in public, but who was weakened by an inner lack of confidence, falling for Iago's lies because he could not believe that Desdemona really loved him.

OTHELLO THE MOOR

A Moor is someone who comes from north-west Africa (mainly present-day Morocco and Tunisia). However, it is possible that the word in Shakespeare's time could have been used for any African, and today Othello is most often played by actors with black African rather than Arab features.

For centuries Othello was played by white actors wearing black make-up. The first black actor to play Othello was Ira Aldridge, an American who performed the role in England in 1825. Another black American, Paul Robeson, played Othello in London in 1930 and then at the Royal Shakespeare Theatre, Stratford-upon-Avon in 1959. After that, no black actor played Othello at the **RSC** until Willard White in 1989 (although Ben Kingsley, whose father was from India, had played him as a North African Arab in the 1985 **RSC** production).

Since the 1990s, no major white actor has 'blacked up' to play Othello on the British stage. However, there was an interesting experiment in 1998 at the **Shakespeare Theater, Washington, D.C.,** when the British actor Patrick Stewart played the part as a white man in a cast that was mainly black. He felt that this allowed predominantly white audiences to look afresh at the racism in the play by putting themselves in Othello's place. Many actors take the view that it doesn't matter what colour Othello is, or what ethnic background he has; the important thing is that he is seen to be sufficiently different from the Venetians to be the subject of racism.

There are some black actors who refuse to play the part. Hugh Quarshie, for example, argues that the play encourages white audiences to view all black men as over-emotional and unstable. However, others feel that Othello behaves as he does not because he is black, but because he has had little experience with women, and is over-trusting and too easily made jealous.

IAGO'S MOTIVES

Why does Iago behave so wickedly? Is he bitter that he has not been made lieutenant, jealous that other men have slept with his wife, or does he simply love destroying other people's happiness? David Suchet, in the 1985 **RSC** production, believed that Iago's problem was that he had a passionate love for Othello and felt let down when Cassio was chosen as lieutenant. In **Parker**'s 1995 film, Kenneth Branagh takes a similar approach; he weeps as he clings to Othello and tells him 'I am your own for ever'. Ian McKellen's Iago at the **RSC** in 1989 seemed eaten up by jealousy – jealous of his wife's supposed relationships with other men and jealous of the happy marriage enjoyed by Othello and Desdemona. Michael MacLiammóir in **Welles**'s 1952 film comes across as simply an evil man who wants to destroy the happiness of others.

The audience can learn much about Iago's motives from watching how he speaks his soliloquies. Ian McKellen was almost overcome with passion when he said 'I hate the Moor'. Kenneth Branagh's Iago seems to want us to understand how hurt he is by Othello and speaks every soliloquy straight to camera, as though sharing secrets with a friend.

PLAYING THE WOMEN

Because Othello and Iago are such powerful characters, there is a danger that the women can be overlooked in this play. Desdemona in particular can come across as simply a weak victim who allows Othello to insult her and push her around. In **Parker**'s 1995 film, Irène Jacob never really fights back, even at the end. In contrast, Imogen Stubbs's Desdemona in the 1989 **RSC** production was a strong character throughout, and desperately struggled to escape from the room when she realised that Othello intended to kill her. Suzanne Cloutier also fights bravely against her murderer in **Welles**'s 1952 film: as the sheet is pressed tighter and tighter over her face, her features strain beneath it like a ghost in a horror movie.

In many productions Iago and Emila have a bad relationship. In the 1995 **Parker** film Emilia is a sad figure, abused by her violent husband. Zoë Wanamaker's Emilia, at the **RSC** in 1989, was so jealous of Desdemona's happy marriage that she gave the handkerchief to Iago knowing how much trouble its loss would cause. But when at the end she realised what Iago had done, she showed amazing courage in revealing the truth and accepting her own part in the tragedy.

The third woman in the play, Bianca, has sometimes been portrayed as a prostitute or 'courtesan', but usually she seems to be simply someone Cassio has met since his arrival on Cyprus. Often portrayed as dark-skinned, showing that she is an inhabitant of Cyprus rather than Venice, she usually comes across as a free spirit with an outgoing personality, in contrast to Desdemona who has had a sheltered upbringing, and the often sad figure of Emilia.

STAGING AND SETTING

Film makers have used a variety of locations to bring out the themes of *Othello*. In his 1952 film, **Welles** uses cramped tunnels, low ceilings and patterns of light and shade to create a cage-like world in which Othello is gradually being trapped. Many the images in **Parker**'s 1995 film are of the sea, with powerful waves crashing against rocks. This mirrors Othello's stormy emotions and also reminds the audience of his claim that his bloody thoughts, 'Like to the Pontic Sea', will never let him turn back until his revenge is complete.

Many stage productions, such as the 2004 **RSC** production, have dressed the men in military uniforms throughout, a constant reminder that they are professional soldiers. This helps us to understand why Othello might be so easily deceived by Iago. Firstly, given that Othello has been a soldier since he was seven, it is hardly surprising if he lacks any deep knowledge of women. Secondly, Iago has fought alongside him in many battles, which makes him the kind of reliable comrade a professional soldier would always trust.

ASSESSMENT OF SHAKESPEARE IN YOUR ENGLISH LITERATURE GCSE

All students studying GCSE English Literature have to study at least six texts, three of which are from the English, Welsh or Irish literary heritage. These texts must include prose, poetry and drama, and in England this must include a play by Shakespeare.

The four major exam boards: AQA, Edexcel, WJEC and OCR, include Shakespeare as part of their specifications for English Literature. All the exam boards offer controlled assessment to assess their students' understanding of Shakespeare, although some offer a traditional examination as an alternative option, or as one element of the assessment.

This section of the book offers guidance and support to help you prepare for your GCSE assessment on Shakespeare. The first part (pages 258–60) is relevant to all students, whichever exam board's course you are taking. The second part (pages 261–76) is board-specific, and you should turn to those pages that are relevant to your exam board. Your teacher will advise you if you are unsure which board you are working with.

WHAT YOU WILL BE ASSESSED ON

In your English Literature GCSE you will be marked on various Assessment Objectives (AOs). These assess your ability to:

- **AO1: respond to texts critically and imaginatively; select and evaluate relevant textual detail to illustrate and support interpretations**
  This means that you should show insight and imagination when writing about the text, showing understanding of what the author is saying and how he or she is saying it; and use quotations or direct references to the text to support your ideas and point of view.

- **AO2: explain how language, structure and form contribute to writers' presentation of ideas, themes and settings**
  This means that you need to explain how writers use language (vocabulary, imagery and other literary features), structure and form (the 'shape' of the text) to present ideas, themes and settings (where the action takes place).

- **AO3: make comparisons and explain links between texts, evaluating writers' different ways of expressing meaning and achieving effects**
  This means that you need to compare and link texts, identifying what they have in common and looking at how different writers express meaning and create specific effects for the reader/audience.

- **AO4: relate texts to their social, cultural and historical contexts; explain how texts have been influential and significant to self and other readers in different contexts and at different times**
  This means that, where it is relevant, you need to show awareness of the social, cultural and historical background of the texts; explain the influence of texts on yourself and other readers in different places and times.

You will also be assessed on the **Quality of your Written Communication**. This means you need to ensure that: your text is legible and your spelling, punctuation and grammar are accurate so that the meaning is clear; you choose a style of writing that is suitable for the task; you organise information clearly and logically, using specialist words where relevant.

Not all exam boards assess all the AOs as part of the English Literature Shakespeare task. Here is a summary:

Exam Board	Unit	AO1	AO2	AO3	AO4
AQA	Unit 3 CA	✓	✓	✓	✓
Edexcel	Unit 3 CA		✓	✓	
WJEC	Unit 2 Exam	✓	✓		✓

WHAT IS CONTROLLED ASSESSMENT?

Controlled assessment is a way of testing students' knowledge and ability. It differs from an examination in that you will be given the task in advance so you can research and prepare for it, before sitting down to write a full response to it under supervised conditions.

Exam boards differ in the detail of their controlled assessment rules, so do check them out in the board-specific section. However, the general stages of controlled assessment are as follows:

1. The task

Every year exam boards either set a specific task or offer a choice. Your teacher might adapt one of the tasks to suit you and the resources available. You will be given this task well in advance of having to respond to it, so you have plenty of time to prepare for it.

2. Planning and research

Your teacher will have helped you study your text and taught you how to approach the topics. He or she will now advise you on how to carry out further research and plan for your task.

- During this phase you can work with others, for example discussing ideas and sharing resources on the internet.

- Your teacher can give you general feedback during this phase, but not detailed advice.

- You must keep a record of all the source materials you use, including websites.

3. Writing up the response

This will take place under timed, supervised conditions.

- It may be split into more than one session, in which case your teacher will collect your work at the end of the session and put it away until the beginning of the next. You will not have access to it between sessions.

- You may be allowed to take an **un-annotated copy** of the text into the session.

- You may be allowed to take in some brief **notes**.

- You may be allowed access to a **dictionary** or a **thesaurus**.

- You may be allowed to produce your assessment electronically, but you will not be allowed access to the internet, email, disks or memory sticks.

- During this time, you may not communicate with other candidates. The work you produce must be entirely **your own**.

- Your teacher will advise you on how much you should aim to write.

4. Marking

Your Controlled Assessment Task will be marked by your teacher and may be moderated (supervised and checked) by your exam board.

General examiners' note

Remember:

- you will get marks for responding to the task, but not for writing other material that is not relevant

- you must produce an **individual** response to the task in the final assessment, even if you have discussed ideas with other students previously.

How to succeed in AQA English Literature

If you are studying *Othello* for AQA your knowledge and understanding of the play will be tested in a Controlled Assessment Task. In this task you will have to write about Othello and one other text that your teacher will choose. This other text may be a novel, a selection of poetry, another play, or even another Shakespeare play. The two texts will be linked in some way and you need to write about both in detail.

> ### Examiner's tip
> You will be assessed on the following objectives when responding to your Shakespeare task: AO1, AO2, AO3, AO4. Refer back to pages 258–9 for more about these assessment objectives.

The task

AQA will give your teacher a number of tasks to choose from. There are two main topics:

1. Themes and ideas

This might mean writing about love or loyalty, revenge or jealousy, racism or prejudice. For example: *Explore the ways writers present and use the ideas of loyalty in the texts you have studied* **or** *Explore the ways writers have presented love and jealousy in the texts you have studied.*

2. Characterisation and voice

This might mean writing about relationships, young and old characters, or heroes and villains. For example: *Explore the ways texts show characters changing under the influence of others* **or** *Explore the ways in which villains are presented in texts you have studied.*

Your response

- You have to complete a written response to ONE task. This should be about 2,000 words but remember that it's quality not quantity that counts.

- You have FOUR hours to produce your work. Your teacher will probably ask you to complete the task over separate sessions rather than in a single sitting.

- Your teacher will give you plenty of time to prepare for the task. You can use any resources you like, but do keep a record of them (including websites). You must include a list of these at the end of your task.

- You can work in a small group to research and prepare your material but your final work must be all your own.

- Do watch different versions of the play. You can refer to the different versions when you write your response and you will be given credit for this.

- You can refer to brief notes when you are writing your response, but these must be brief. You must hand in your notes at the end of each session and on completion of the task. You can also use a copy of the play without any annotations.

- You can handwrite your response or use a word processor. You are allowed a dictionary and thesaurus or grammar and spell-check programs. You are NOT allowed to use the internet, email, disks or memory sticks when writing your response.

- You can do the Controlled Assessment Task in January or June. When you have finished, your teachers will mark your work and then send a sample from your school to AQA to be checked.

Examiner's tip

The Controlled Assessment is worth 25 per cent of your final English Literature mark – so it's worth doing it well.

HOW TO GET A GOOD GRADE

1. Select what you write about carefully. It is better to write a lot about a little. Concentrate on one scene in Shakespeare and one chapter in a novel or a single poem, or on two characters, one from a Shakespeare play and one from a novel.

2. Use short, relevant quotations. Every time you include a quotation, consider the language the writer has used and the probable effect on the audience.

3. Never retell the story. You and your teachers already know it. If you find yourself doing this, stop and refocus on the question.

4. Check your spellings, in particular writers' and characters' names.

5. Always remember that Othello, Iago, Desdemona and Emilia, and all the other characters in the play are not real. Do not write about them as if they are. They have been created by Shakespeare: his play is the important thing to consider.

SAMPLE CONTROLLED ASSESSMENT TASK

> Explore the ways writers present characters with a flaw which leads to their destruction.

Here and on the following page are extracts from responses written by two students. Both are writing about Othello's speech before he kills Desdemona, in Act 5 Scene 2.

Extract 1 – Grade C response

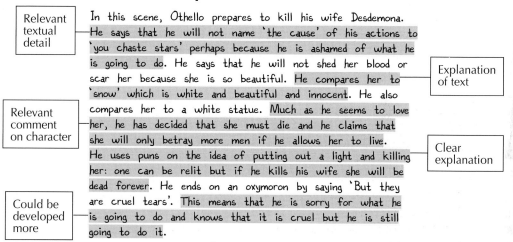

Relevant textual detail

Relevant comment on character

Could be developed more

Explanation of text

Clear explanation

In this scene, Othello prepares to kill his wife Desdemona. He says that he will not name 'the cause' of his actions to 'you chaste stars' perhaps because he is ashamed of what he is going to do. He says that he will not shed her blood or scar her because she is so beautiful. He compares her to 'snow' which is white and beautiful and innocent. He also compares her to a white statue. Much as he seems to love her, he has decided that she must die and he claims that she will only betray more men if he allows her to live. He uses puns on the idea of putting out a light and killing her: one can be relit but if he kills his wife she will be dead forever. He ends on an oxymoron by saying 'But they are cruel tears'. This means that he is sorry for what he is going to do and knows that it is cruel but he is still going to do it.

Examiner's comments

- The ideas here are expressed clearly and appropriately.
- The student has a good understanding of the text and demonstrates how Shakespeare has used linguistic devices such as comparisons, a pun and an oxymoron. These examples are sensibly explained.
- There is evidence of a personal response in the comments that Othello still seems to love Desdemona and also in his realisation that he is being cruel while being determined to kill her.
- In order to raise the grade, the student needs to develop ideas in more detail, including more consideration of Shakespeare's use of language, and also to consider the possible effects this speech would have on an audience.
- As it stands this is a Grade C response.

Extract 2 – Grade A response

Clear use of detail

Analysis linked to theme

Sophisticated insight into theme

Sensitive exploration of theme

Detailed analysis

Othello's torment is a lingering one. He intends to kill his wife in cold blood but Shakespeare makes it appear that he might change his mind. 'It is the cause' he repeats to himself, as though trying to justify what he is about to do. However, such suspense is short-lived. He is intent on a tragically mistaken revenge. Iago has finally triumphed: Othello has become a crudely racist figure – the black man entering the white girl's bedroom to kill her. Shakespeare emphasises the nature of the killing by referring to Desdemona's 'whiter skin' and, in highly measured polysyllabic words, uses the simile 'smooth as monumental alabaster'. Here Desdemona's whiteness is linked both to the idea of statuesque beauty and of death: the monument will be on her tomb. The language of black and white is then further developed by the contrast of light and dark. Othello can put out one light (the physical light) and then restore it; should he put out the figurative light (Desdemona) he will have killed her. Once again Shakespeare makes the audience aware of the racial differences between them: as Iago sneers at Brabantio 'the old black ram' and 'your white ewe'.

Examiner's comments

- In this response the ideas are expressed cogently and persuasively and text references are apt.
- There is evidence of imagination in the development of the interpretation and there is a confident exploration of Shakespeare's use of language; for example, in the exploration of the significance of 'monumental alabaster'.
- The student has written a lot about a little and has also managed to link this to a consideration of the ideas which can be found in the whole text, exploring some of the play's themes and showing awareness that Othello is Shakespeare's dramatic construct.
- This is an example of a Grade A response.

How to succeed in Edexcel English Literature

The response to Shakespeare in Edexcel GCSE English Literature is a Controlled Assessment Task. You must produce your work at school or college under supervision and within two hours, although you may do some preparation for it in advance.

The task

The task will ask you to compare and make links between your own reading of the Shakespeare text and an adaptation. The adaptation can be a film, TV production, musical, graphic novel, audio version or a cartoon, but all must be based on the original play. The task will focus on **one** of the following aspects of the play:

- **Characterisation**
  For example, a study of the importance and development of one of the main characters in the play.

- **Stagecraft**
  For example, looking at ways in which the decisions taken about the staging and set influence the production.

- **Theme**
  For example, following how the action of the play is affected by a central theme such as love, jealous or betrayal.

- **Relationships**
  For example, between Othello and Iago or Othello and Desdemona.

Note that your answer should include some discussion of dramatic devices. These include a range of theatrical techniques and styles used by the playwright to create a particular effect on the audience, such as soliloquies, monologues; juxtaposition and contrast; use of dramatic irony; use of the stage and props; actions and reactions.

Preparing your response

When preparing, you will be able to use a range of resources available at your centre, which may include the internet, TV, videos and film, live performances and notes made in class.

You must complete your tasks individually, without intervention or assistance from others. However, you will be able to use:

- copies of the text without any annotations written in them
- notes (bullet or numbered points), but not a prepared draft or continuous phrases/sentences or paragraphs)
- a dictionary or thesaurus
- grammar or spell-check programs.

Examiner's tip

If possible, see several different adaptations of *Othello* and compare the way they treat the story and characters.

How to get a good grade

To get a good mark in this response, it is important that you:

- respond to the chosen drama text critically and imaginatively
- make comparisons and explain links with your own reading
- look at different ways that a production or adaptation expresses ideas
- consider what Shakespeare means and how he achieves his effects
- support your ideas by including evidence from the words of the play.

Activities

The following approaches will help you to explore *Othello* in preparation for the controlled assessment.

Activity 1: Characterisation

Draw up a page with two columns, one for Iago, one for Cassio. Look at how we find out more about them. Note down key headings, which may be the same for each, such as status, what motivated them, attitudes to each other, and attitudes to Othello. Develop your ideas, support them with brief references, and compare them with a performance of *Othello*.

Activity 2: Stagecraft

In a group, plan the production of a performance of *Othello*. Give each member of the group a non-acting role in the production, such as being responsible for production, costume and make-up, props, lighting, sound, or set design. Decide on the most important decisions or tasks each member has to undertake and make notes on each.

Activity 3: Theme

As you study *Othello* decide on two important themes (e.g. jealousy and loyalty), and note down moments in the play that deal with these. Give brief references from the text that support them.

Activity 4: Relationships

While working through *Othello*, focus on the relationship between Othello and Desdemona. Draw up a page with two columns, noting down headings for your ideas about the relationship in the first column, e.g. the importance of Desdemona, military prowess, the effects of jealousy, love and distrust. In the second column write down references from the text, using key words and phrases.

SAMPLE CONTROLLED ASSESSMENT TASK

- Choose one key theme in the Shakespeare drama text you have studied.
- Compare your reading of the theme with the presentation of the same theme in an adaptation.
- Use examples from the text in your response.

Here and on the following pages are extracts from essays by two candidates who had each watched a modern re-make of *Othello*, the film *O*, and compared this with their own reading of the play.

Extract 1 – Grade C response

Clearly sets out the theme

The play Othello is full of jealousy. Iago is jealous of Othello because he is a general even though he is a Moor, and also because Othello promoted Cassio, not him. Because Iago is jealous himself, he knows it will have the biggest effect on Othello. Shakespeare shows how jealousy leads to evil, unless you can control it. Several times he compares jealousy to a disease or a monster, with Iago saying 'I'll pour this pestilence into his ear', and 'the green-eyed monster'.

Good point as to why Iago decides to work on Othello's jealousy

Explains links between two versions

In the film O, it is jealousy that makes the characters act badly too. Instead of Venice, this is set in an American high school and the director has switched wars and generals for high school team sports. Hugo (Iago) is jealous that O/Odin (Othello) is the captain of the basketball team, not him. Because this might not seem enough to make him want to bring down Othello, this version also has the basketball coach being Hugo's dad who seems to prefer Odin to Hugo. He says 'I love him like my own son'. Before any of the tragic events have happened in Shakespeare's play, Othello hints that bad things are to come: 'When I love thee not, / Chaos is come'.

Evidence of interpretation of film

In both versions, there is lots of chaos. Hugo knows that, just as when Shakespeare wrote Othello, a man's weaknesses are his pride and his feelings about his woman. At the beginning of the play, Othello said of Desdemona, 'My life upon her faith!'. This turned out to be truer than he first thought as he ends up killing her and also himself. In O, Odin's jealousy is made worse by taking drugs, but he also ends up killing Desi (Desdemona) and himself too.

A key point, but needs developing

Needs explanation rather then narration

Examiner's comments

- The candidate clearly evaluates different ways of expressing meaning, by comparisons between the two versions.
- The theme is dealt with appropriately, and the examples support the points about the effects of jealousy.
- Explanations are sound. To achieve a higher grade, the candidate would need to go into greater detail and analysis of the examples. Several points are simply stated, without a real sense of why they are important. Also, some relevant quotations are included but without really explaining their significance to the theme.
- As it stands, this is a Grade C response.

Extract 2 – Grade A response

Effective comment on importance of the theme

When reading Othello, it is easy to see that jealousy motivates many of the main plot issues. It is the theme of jealousy that unifies the characters. When we are first introduced to Iago, we know it is his jealousy of Othello's position in society that leads him to form his initial plan; he therefore understands the potency of jealousy in others. Even though Desdemona is set up as entirely pure, not only by Othello, but by others, like Roderigo ('She's full of most blessed condition'), Iago is sure that he will be able to use only 'trifles light as air' and 'as little a web as this' to allow the fires of jealousy to burn in Othello.

Good knowledge of text, interwoven effectively

The director of O, a modern filmed adaptation, has changed the words and the setting, but we know that the story is essentially the same. He has changed the metaphor of warfare to the battles of high-school sports teams and Desdemona (now Desi) is the daughter of the Principal and the most popular girl in school. However, it is still jealousy that makes Hugo (Iago) so angry at Odin, nicknamed O. The theme of jealousy is used, in both the original and the adaptation, to act both as the hunter and the web to ensnare the main characters. Desdemona's fateful handkerchief even has 'magic in the web of it', whereas the webbed motif could be suggested by the webbing of the basketball nets in the film O.

Clear explanation of how modern version has used old ideas

Perceptive point linking language to visual effects

One difference is that in Othello, the rage and jealousy themselves are enough to lead Othello to murder: they 'ensnared my soul and body'. In O, this has to be slightly changed. The fear of cuckoldry may still be as potent, but it is no longer acceptable socially that a cheating woman will be so harshly punished. Here, O's jealous rages are fuelled by a past with hard drugs that resurfaces in his anger and increase his paranoia to the level that he murders the woman he loves.

Strong, well-articulated personal viewpoint

Explanation of effect of character's use of drugs

Examiner's comments

- This is a very promising extract, which offers 'discriminating comparisons and links showing insight', as required for the highest band of marks.
- The writer has demonstrated excellent awareness of language and structure, as well as a strong personal response to both the text and the film.
- The reader is drawn into the candidate's interpretation in such a way as to wish to see how this modern version reworks the theme of jealousy.
- This is a Grade A response.

How to succeed in WJEC English Literature

Othello is one of the set drama texts for Unit 2a (Literary heritage drama and contemporary prose) in the exam.

The examination question will be in two parts. The first part will focus on an extract from the play, which is printed in the question paper. Your response will be worth 10 marks. The second part will consist of a choice of two essays. You will choose one question to answer and your response will be worth 20 marks.

You should spend about 20 minutes on your response to the printed extract, and about 40 minutes on the essay.

The extract question

The extract is always the same for both Higher and Foundation tiers. The questions are similar, but the Foundation question will be rather more straightforward, with more emphasis on 'what' rather than 'how', and will be more likely to remind you of the need to support your answer with words and phrases from the extract.

Typical Higher tier questions are:

> • With close reference to the extract, show how Shakespeare creates mood and atmosphere for an audience here.
>
> • Look closely at how Othello speaks and behaves here. What does it reveal about his state of mind?

Typical Foundation tier questions are:

> • What do you think of the way Othello and Iago speak and behave here? Give reasons for what you say, and remember to support your answer with words and phrases from the extract.
>
> • How do you think an audience would respond to this part of the play? Remember to support your answer with reference to the extract.

Activities

• You may find it helpful to practise for your examination by choosing one or more of the above questions, selecting a key extract from *Othello* (about a page in length) and preparing notes on how you would answer it.

How to get a good grade

Before you start responding to the extract question, think carefully:

- Take note of the question and decide exactly what it is asking for (i.e. your interpretation of the extract) – this will form the basis of your response. Make sure that you can support your views with close reference to the text.

- Be prepared to put the extract in context (i.e. show you understand how the extract fits into the play as a whole). This could be a useful starting point for your response.

- As you read the extract, underline key words and phrases that support your interpretation. It's important to cover the whole of the extract – there will be a very good reason why it starts and ends where it does, so make sure you go right to the end. Try to select details from the beginning, the middle and the end, and then from key points in between.

As you start **writing** your response:

- Make sure you have a strong opening, and make specific points right from the start. For example, if the question asks you to discuss the mood and atmosphere in the extract, say what the mood and atmosphere is, in your opinion. Or, if the question asks you for your thoughts and feelings about a character, make your point of view clear in the first couple of sentences.

- As you make points, keep referring back to the question, so that you keep focused.

- For every point you make, prove it with evidence from the extract. Aim to keep the evidence brief. Long quotations don't earn you any more marks, and give you less time to discuss your points.

- Explain how your evidence or selected detail supports the point you have made. (Some people use the expression **PEE**, or **P**oint, **E**vidence, **E**xplanation, to remind them about this.)

> Look closely at how Iago and Cassio speak and behave here. What does it reveal about their relationship?
>
> **Extract: Act 2 Scene 3, lines 245–293 (pages 95 to 97)**
>
> IAGO   What, are you hurt, lieutenant?
>
>   …
>
> IAGO   Come, come, good wine is a good familiar creature if it be well used. Exclaim no more against it.

Here and on the following pages are extracts from essays by students.

Extract 1 – Grade C response

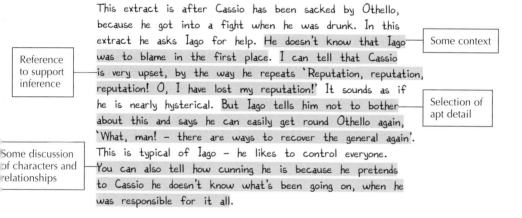

This extract is after Cassio has been sacked by Othello, because he got into a fight when he was drunk. In this extract he asks Iago for help. **He doesn't know that Iago was to blame in the first place.** I can tell that Cassio is very upset, by the way he repeats 'Reputation, reputation, reputation! O, I have lost my reputation!' It sounds as if he is nearly hysterical. But Iago tells him not to bother about this and says he can easily get round Othello again, 'What, man! – there are ways to recover the general again'. This is typical of Iago – he likes to control everyone. You can also tell how cunning he is because he pretends to Cassio he doesn't know what's been going on, when he was responsible for it all.

Labels (left and right margins):
- Reference to support inference
- Some discussion of characters and relationships
- Some context
- Selection of apt detail

Examiner's comments

- There is clear awareness of what is going on here.

- There is some discussion of characters and relationships.

- To improve this response, the student needs to discuss the way the characters speak and behave in greater detail. More focus on individual words or phrases would also be worthwhile.

- As it stands, this is a Grade C response.

Extract 2 – Grade A response

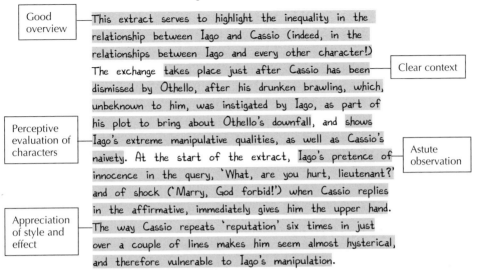

Good overview

This extract serves to highlight the inequality in the relationship between Iago and Cassio (indeed, in the relationships between Iago and every other character!) The exchange takes place just after Cassio has been dismissed by Othello, after his drunken brawling, which, unbeknown to him, was instigated by Iago, as part of his plot to bring about Othello's downfall, and shows Iago's extreme manipulative qualities, as well as Cassio's naivety. At the start of the extract, Iago's pretence of innocence in the query, 'What, are you hurt, lieutenant?' and of shock ('Marry, God forbid!') when Cassio replies in the affirmative, immediately gives him the upper hand. The way Cassio repeats 'reputation' six times in just over a couple of lines makes him seem almost hysterical, and therefore vulnerable to Iago's manipulation.

Clear context

Perceptive evaluation of characters

Astute observation

Appreciation of style and effect

Examiner's comments

- This is a well-focused and perceptive start to a response.
- There is clear evidence of overview and evaluation.
- All points made are well-supported by reference to the text.
- There is evidence of close reading and sensitive probing of the subtext.
- This is a Grade A response.

RESPONDING TO THE ESSAY QUESTION

For the longer, essay-style response, you will have a choice of questions. It is important to choose the one you feel you can do best. There is usually at least one about a character or characters, and other types of questions may focus on themes or on a particular part of the play (for example, why it is important to the play as a whole.)

As you **write** your essay, make sure you:

- have a good strong start, with clear reference to the question
- keep focused on the question throughout (a reference to it in every paragraph is a good idea)
- show the examiner you know the play in detail, but don't worry about long quotations – the shorter and more direct the reference the better
- select key parts of the play (and make sure you refer to the whole play, including its ending)
- have a clear and specific conclusion, summing up your main ideas.

Usually, the questions for Higher and Foundation tiers will be on similar topics. The difference between the tiers is that those on the Foundation tier are more likely to have bullet points to help you organise your answer, and/or to be worded in a more straightforward way. To get a good mark on the Foundation tier, it is important to use all the bullet points to help you frame your answer. Higher tier questions will have more focus on 'how', and are less likely to have bullet points. On both tiers, you must be sure to show your knowledge of the **whole** play.

A typical Higher tier question might be:

> Why does Othello kill Desdemona?

Or,

> How does Shakespeare present the character Iago to an audience throughout the play?

A typical Foundation tier question might be:

> At the beginning of the play, Othello loves and marries Desdemona; at the end of the play he kills her. Write about some of the important turning points in their relationship that led to this tragic end.

Or,

> Write about Iago.
>
> Think about:
> - his relationship with Othello
> - his relationships with other characters
> - the way he speaks and behaves at different points in the play.

SAMPLE HIGHER TIER EXAMINATION QUESTION AND RESPONSES

> Why does Othello kill Desdemona?

Extract 1 – Grade C response

Apt focus on the relationship

At the beginning of the play, Desdemona and Othello are in love. Desdemona must love Othello very much because she runs away with him and marries him without her father's permission, which was a bad thing in those days, and then when Iago tells him what has happened she defends him when everyone seems to be against him and is calling him names, like Roderigo calling him 'a lascivious Moor', which is not only racist, but suggests all Othello wants is sex. Brabantio, Desdemona's father, is really angry because he thinks Othello has put a spell on her or otherwise she could not love him. This is because he is black and she is white, he is a soldier and she is a lady, and also because he is older than her.

Discussion of selected detail

Some discussion of context

Valid reference to events

So Othello has to tell the Duke of Venice and Brabantio and all the officials how they met and fell in love. He says that Brabantio liked hearing Othello's stories of his early life and travels and then Desdemona got interested and soon they fell in love. When Desdemona has a chance to speak she explains that Othello is now her husband and she will be loyal to him. Othello's speech has convinced the Duke, 'I think this tale would win my daughter too,' and Brabantio, still rather reluctantly, accepts their marriage. After this, Othello goes to defend Cyprus and Desdemona asks if she can go with him, 'Let me go with him.' This again shows she loves him.

Reference, but could develop further

Well-chosen quotation to support point

Sensible inference

Examiner's comments

- This opening response is engaged and shows a clear awareness of the relationship between the characters at this point in the play.
- There are some relevant references to the text to support the points being made.
- To achieve a higher grade, more focus on the significance of specific words and phrases would be useful, such as in the speech of Othello defending his actions. More developed discussion of the way the characters speak and behave would also improve the response, as it tends to re-tell events, and only focuses on specific detail for some of the time.
- As it stands, this is a Grade C response.

Extract 2 – Grade A response

Othello's final words in the play, as he commits suicide, are:

'I kissed thee ere I killed thee. No way but this,

Killing myself, to die upon a kiss.'

| Clear context, focus and overview |

These words spoken to the body of his wife, Desdemona, whom he has just smothered, at the suggestion of the ironically described 'honest Iago', sum up the complexity of Othello's feelings for her. At the start of the play, they had overcome huge obstacles to be together. Their courtship had thrived despite differences in age, status, background and race, yet the prescient final words of Brabantio, Desdemona's father, to Othello:

| Succinct overview |

| Apt reference |

'Look to her, Moor, if thou hast eyes to see:

She has deceived her father, and may thee'

may have sown the seeds for Othello's growing insecurity, which is fostered and fed by Iago, for his own motives. Iago acknowledges in a soliloquy:

| Astute inference |

'The Moor is of a free and open nature,

That thinks men honest that but seem to be so –

And will as tenderly be led by the nose

As asses are.'

| Language and effect |

Iago's use of animal imagery, comparing his superior in a dismissive and derogatory manner as an 'ass', highlights his disdain for Othello, and he proceeds to play upon his insecurities in order to destroy him. Getting him to destroy Desdemona, with whom Othello was so in love, seems a necessary step in Iago's plot, and Othello, the 'ass' is lead to his fate.

| Evaluation of characters and relationships |

Examiner's comments

- This opening response has plenty of high-grade indicators from the start. There is a clear overview of the relationship and evaluation of the behaviour of key characters.

- The technique of starting with reference to the ending of the play makes the overview particularly evident.

- Direct reference to the text is well handled, in the form of aptly chosen quotations, and there is clear appreciation of language and its effects.

- Thoughtful and sensitive exploration of the dynamics of the relationships is evident throughout.

- This is a strong Grade A response.